AI as a Guide, Not a Judge

Real-World Lessons from Deploying AI in the Justice System

Aaron Judy

This book is for informational purposes only and does not constitute legal advice.

ISBN 979-8-9965009-0-1 (paperback)

ISBN 979-8-9965009-1-8 (ebook)

Published by Neverworks Press

Trademarks and Disclaimers:

All product names, logos, and brands mentioned in this book are property of their respective owners. All company, product, and service names used in this book are for identification purposes only. Use of these names, trademarks, and brands does not imply endorsement or sponsorship. The views and opinions expressed in this book are solely those of the author and do not reflect the official policy or position of any mentioned employer or company.

Dedication

For those who never made it to the courthouse door.

Preface

This book grew out of a problem I could not solve with a single conversation.

When I was implementing AI inside one of the largest court systems in the country, I kept having two completely different conversations at the same time. One conversation was with my leadership, who needed to understand *why* any of this mattered, what the risks were, and what would happen if we got it wrong. The other conversation was with my implementation team, who needed to understand *how* to actually build it—the architecture decisions, the failure modes, the things that look good in a demo and break in production.

Those two conversations are both in this book. I wrote it that way on purpose. Chopping out the technical depth would have robbed practitioners of the honest account they need. Removing the human stakes would have left leaders with another technology brief that explains features without explaining consequences.

If you are a court administrator, judge, policymaker, or subcommittee member: every chapter has something for you. The sections labeled "Our Implementation" and the more technical subsections on system architecture are written primarily for builders; feel free to skim them. But I encourage you not to skip Chapter 7. The risks in the second half of that chapter are the ones that will land on your desk, not your IT director's.

If you are a court technologist, AI implementer, or vendor: do not skip the first two chapters because they seem philosophical. The "why" of Access to Justice is not backdrop; it is the constraint that should drive every design decision you make. If you understand what is at stake for the person on the other side of your system, you will build it differently.

A note on how I wrote this: everything in the "Our Implementation" sections happened. The numbers are real. The failures are real. The man who rushed through security only to discover he was in the wrong building—he is real, too. I have changed no outcomes and invented no successes. The point of including those specifics is not to impress; it is to give you something concrete to stand on when someone in your organization asks whether any of this actually works.

The dedication at the front of this book is for people who never made it to the courthouse door. This preface is for everyone who can change that.

Aaron Judy

Table of Contents

Chapter 1 Access to Justice

Rural America

I grew up in Appalachia, in a community where people did not trust the law, and the nearest courthouse was over an hour's drive through the mountains. For many families, that meant justice was not just delayed, it was unreachable. Distance, cost, and fear did not just make things harder; they stopped people before they ever tried.

Even geography shaped perception. The law felt like it belonged somewhere else, not to us. It created a quiet but persistent divide: us versus them.

When the law *was* on the mountain, word traveled fast. People had police scanners. There was an informal network that let everyone know. I remember my father warning me about tattoos. Not for religious reasons, but because if I ever got in trouble, that is how they would identify me. I would never be able to run.

It is questionable advice. But it captures the sentiment.

Those early experiences shaped my understanding of Access to Justice and why I believe technology can help bridge that gap. Despite that upbringing and years of learned mistrust, I ended up working inside the judicial branch of one of the largest counties in the country. Something my younger self would never have believed.

Access to justice means different things depending on your trust, your needs, and your lived experience. But too often, we define it too narrowly. We focus on the courtroom. We assume presence is enough. We insist the litigant find impossible funding for representation when they worry about the hours of work they will miss or the coinage for the parking meter.

For many people, the gate never even opens.

Why Access to Justice

Justice is often depicted as a blindfolded goddess holding scales. We are told the law is neutral, that rules apply to everyone equally. But an invisible wall stands between the letter of the law and the lives of the people it is meant to protect. That wall is built out of complexity, cost, and language.

When we talk about **Access to Justice (A2J)**, we are talking about the ability of any person, regardless of their bank account, their education, or the language they speak, to use the legal system to solve their problems.

The Cost of Silence

When a person cannot access the justice system, their problems don't go away; they multiply.

An unresolved wrongful eviction does not stay an eviction. It becomes homelessness, a night in a car, children pulled from school, a job lost. The legal problem that could have been addressed became a cascading life crisis because the person at the center of it couldn't navigate the process that was supposed to protect them.

An inaccessible protection order doesn't stay an administrative gap. It becomes physical danger. Someone who needed the law's protection went without it, not because the law didn't offer it, but because the path to it was too complicated to navigate alone, in the time they had, under the circumstances they were in.

A misunderstood immigration form does not stay a paperwork error. It becomes a fractured family, a deportation, a child left behind. One word misread, one box left blank, one deadline missed. The law had a process. The person couldn't find it.

This is the "Justice Gap." In a perfect world, the law works as a shield. In our world, for many, the law is a maze where the map is written in a language they do not speak, and the "exit" requires a fee they cannot pay.

Justice as a Public Utility

We often think of justice as something found only in a courtroom. But justice is a **public utility**, much like clean water or electricity. You should not need a specialized degree or a high-priced consultant just to "turn the lights on."

Access to justice means:

1. **Knowing your rights:** Awareness that a legal solution even exists.
2. **Navigating the system:** The ability to file the right paperwork in the right place.
3. **Meaningful Participation:** Being able to tell your story and be heard without a "second of exclusion."

The Digital Bridge

This is where the technology discussed in this book enters the frame. If the wall is built of complexity, generative AI, agentic systems, and real-time translation are the tools we use to dismantle it. We are not just making things "faster"; we are making them **visible**.

We focus on Access to Justice because **language access is justice access.** If a citizen cannot understand the proceedings against them, the "scales of justice" are not just unbalanced—they are broken.

The Stakes

Government legitimacy rests on one promise: the laws are for everyone. When a large portion of the population is locked out of the legal process, that promise dissolves.

Access to Justice is the difference between a society of **subjects** and a society of **citizens**. A subject has things happen *to* them; a citizen has the power to act *within* the system. This book is about how we use the greatest technological leap of our time to ensure that power belongs to everyone.

The Civil Justice Gap

While the right to an attorney is a hallmark of criminal law, there is no such universal right in civil law. If you are being sued by a debt collector, facing eviction, navigating a custody battle, or fighting a wrongful termination, you are often on your own. The person on the other side of that case almost certainly has legal representation. You have a stack of forms you do not understand and a deadline you cannot miss.

This is where the gap is largest and the stakes are highest. Studies consistently find that in civil cases, outcomes are dramatically better for represented parties than for those who appear alone. The disparity is not primarily about the merits of the case. It is about the ability to navigate the system. A self-represented litigant who doesn't know how to respond to a motion, who misses a procedural deadline, or who doesn't understand what "summary judgment" means may lose not because they were wrong but because the system was designed in a language they were never taught.

This is where AI-driven navigators are not just helpful. They are a lifeline. Not because they replace attorneys, but because they give people the information, the guidance, and the structured support to find the door, walk through it, and show up prepared. That is the minimum a just system owes the people it governs.

Chapter 2 The Barriers

Individuals can struggle with legal literacy, digital literacy, or even traditional reading comprehension despite having higher education.

Language Literacy

Fifty-four percent of U.S. adults are below a sixth-grade reading level.[1] And research shows that reading fear-provoking words, such as "jail," "penalty," and "death," releases hormones that impair reasoning and significantly reduce reading comprehension and diminish trust. In attentional control theory, anxiety impairs the efficient functioning of the goal-directed attentional system and increases the extent to which processing is influenced by the stimulus-driven attentional system.[2]

While the average American reads at a seventh- to eighth-grade level, the average legal document is written at a post-graduate (Grade 17+) level. This ten-year gap is a "Silence Zone" where rights are lost simply because the instructions were unreadable. Bridge-building AI aims to close this ten-year gap instantly. It is our responsibility to meet people where they are, not where we wish they were.

One of the quietest but biggest barriers to justice today is anxiety and neurodiversity. Many people simply cannot navigate a high-pressure in-person or phone interaction. Post-pandemic, a massive portion of the population struggles with synchronous, face-to-face, or phone interactions. Social anxiety is not just "nerves," it is a genuine functional barrier, and neurodiversity layers onto this.

People with ADHD, autism, dyslexia, auditory processing disorders, or executive-function challenges experience the justice system as a

---

[1] National Center for Education Statistics. (2023). *Program for the International Assessment of Adult Competencies (PIAAC): State and county estimates.* U.S. Department of Education. https://nces.ed.gov/surveys/piaac/state-county-estimates.asp

[2] Eysenck, M. W., Derakshan, N., Santos, R., & Calvo, M. G. (2007). Anxiety and cognitive performance: Attentional control theory. *Emotion, 7*(2), 336–353. https://doi.org/10.1037/1528-3542.7.2.336

maze of long forms, ambiguous steps, pressure to "perform" socially, complicated language, and high-stakes interactions. That combination shuts people out before they ever get help. We have to meet people where they are, especially when they are going through the worst moments of their lives.

Legal Literacy

The Language of Power: Demystifying Legal Literacy

The law should not require a degree in Classics just to understand a summons. Yet, for centuries, the legal profession has guarded its gates with a specialized dialect: **Legalese**. While proponents argue that Latin terms and archaic syntax provide precision, in practice, they often serve as a "keep out" sign for the uninitiated.

When a citizen receives a document that says *"Notice of Quia Timet"* or *"Demurrer,"* the system has already failed its first test of literacy. It has prioritized the comfort of the court over the comprehension of the person whose life is being decided.

Portals vs. Bridges

For the last two decades, "improving access" meant building **portals**. We put PDFs online. We made websites with lists of links. We told people, *"The door is open—you just have to find it."* But a portal is useless if you do not have the map to get to the door. Most efforts to improve access still assume that people have already reached the threshold. They assume the citizen knows they have a legal problem, knows which agency handles it, and knows how to "speak" to the portal.

We have to stop building portals and start building bridges.

A bridge meets people where they already are:

- **On their phones:** Not everyone has a laptop or a printer, but almost everyone has a smartphone.

- **In their language:** Not just Spanish or Tagalog, but the "plain language" of everyday life.
- **On their terms:** Providing answers at 11 PM when a parent is finally off work and can address the eviction notice they received that morning.

The "Plain Language" Revolution

Generative AI acts as a **universal translator**, not just between different cultures, but also between "Lawyer" and "Human."

One of the most transformative uses of AI in legal literacy is **Automated Simplification**. Imagine a tool that allows a citizen to take a photo of a dense, three-page court order and asks: *"What does this mean for me?"* The AI does not just summarize; it decodes. It translates *"The Defendant is hereby commanded to appear and show cause"* into *"You must go to the courthouse on Tuesday at 9 AM to explain your side of the story, or you might lose the case automatically."*

Literacy as a Two-Way Street

True literacy is not just the citizen understanding the law; it is the **system understanding the citizen.** When we meet people on their own terms, we allow them to tell their stories in their natural voice. AI-driven interfaces can listen to a rambling, emotional, or non-linear explanation of a problem and extract the "legally salient" facts. This bridges the gap between a person's **lived experience** and the **legal requirements** of a court filing.

The Goal: Functional Autonomy

The end goal of legal literacy is not to turn every citizen into a lawyer. It is to provide them with **functional autonomy**. It is about giving people enough clarity to navigate their lives without fear.

Moving from portals to bridges shifts the burden of "understanding" from the victim to the system. We move from "ignorant of the law" to a world where the law is finally **readable.**

Digital Literacy and the Digital Divide

We often talk about the "Digital Divide" as a matter of hardware: who has a laptop and who has high-speed internet. But there is a second, more insidious divide: **Cognitive Digital Literacy.** For many rural litigants, particularly the elderly, the challenge is not just "getting online"; it is navigating the labyrinth of buttons, drop-down menus, two-factor authentication, and file-upload requirements that characterize modern government portals. When a system is "digital by default," it risks being **"exclusive by design"** for those who did not grow up with a smartphone in their hand.

In many rural areas, "Digital Literacy" is often stunted by "Digital Poverty." When internet speeds are slow, complex portals often "time out" or fail to load. This creates a "Rural Penalty," where a citizen's location dictates their level of legal protection. Agentic AI can help by "batching" tasks locally and uploading them in small, low-bandwidth bursts, ensuring the system works even on a 3G connection.

The Cognitive Load of Crisis

It is important to remember that most people interacting with the justice system are doing so during the worst days of their lives. Under extreme stress, our ability to learn new, complex software drops to near zero. A "simple" three-step upload process can feel like climbing a mountain when you are facing the loss of your farm or your health coverage.

For the elderly, this "cognitive load" is compounded by:

- **Interface Friction:** Tiny fonts, low-contrast buttons, and "hidden" menus that require precise motor skills.

- **The "Fear of the Wrong Click":** A deep-seated anxiety that one accidental press of a button might delete a case or trigger an irreversible legal action.

Moving from "Navigation" to "Conversation"

The solution to limited digital literacy is not more training videos; it is a fundamental shift in **Interface Philosophy**.

Generative AI allows us to move away from "UI" (User Interface) and toward "CI" (Conversational Interface). For a rural litigant who struggles with a mouse and keyboard, the bridge is a **voice-first system.** Instead of navigating a complex website, they can simply speak to their phone: *"I got a paper from the sheriff today. What do I do next?"*

Inclusive Design: Meeting the "Lowest Tech" Standard

To solve for limited digital literacy, we must design for the "lowest tech" common denominator. This means:

1. **Multi-Channel Access:** If a system only works on a high-end iPhone, it is not a public service. It must work via SMS (texting), low-bandwidth web pages, and even landline voice prompts.

2. **The "Grandparent Test":** If a person cannot complete the task without calling a grandchild for help, the interface is too complex.

3. **Human-Assisted Tech:** Digital literacy should not be an "all-or-nothing" proposition. "Bridges" should include "Digital Navigators," real humans at local libraries or post offices who use the AI tools *with* the citizen, providing a handrail for the digital experience.

The Goal: Invisible Technology

The ultimate success of digital literacy in justice is making the technology **invisible**. A citizen should not have to "become a techie" to get a fair shake in court. The technology should work like a glass of water: clear, simple, and essential, without requiring an instruction manual.

The Wearable AI Gap: A New Barrier Inside the Courtroom

The barriers described in this chapter—language, legal literacy, and digital access—mostly exist before the courthouse door. But there is an emerging class of barriers that arise within the proceeding itself, and it is being created not by the court system but by the technology one party brings to the table and the other does not. AI note takers, wearable AI devices, and ambient recording tools are quietly reshaping what it means to be prepared for a hearing. Courts have not yet caught up. The consequences for fairness are real and immediate.

Tools like Otter.ai, Fireflies, and Microsoft Copilot in Teams can join a virtual hearing as a participant, transcribe every word in real time, summarize arguments, flag key statements, and produce a searchable record before the session ends. An attorney using one of these tools during a remote hearing has access to a rolling transcript of everything said. They can review testimony from three minutes ago. They can flag an inconsistency the moment it appears. They can search by keyword during a recess. Their self-represented opponent across the virtual room is working entirely from memory and handwritten notes. That asymmetry is not hypothetical. It is happening in remote hearings right now, in every jurisdiction that moved proceedings online without updating its technology policies.

The physical courtroom presents a harder version of the same problem. Courts have long regulated recording devices, and those rules carry real teeth in most jurisdictions. But the rules were written for cameras, phones, and audio recorders. They were not written for a pair of glasses. Meta Ray-Ban smart glasses can record video and audio, transcribe speech, and surface real-time information to the wearer through a companion app, all without any visible indication that recording is occurring. AI pendant devices like the Limitless Pendant and the Friend can record ambient audio continuously, generate summaries, and flag important moments and are worn around the neck in a way that is indistinguishable from ordinary jewelry. A party wearing either device in a courtroom may be violating existing recording prohibitions, or may not be, depending on how the jurisdiction defines a recording device and whether the rule has been updated since 2015. Most have not been.

The fairness argument cuts in two directions. When only one party has access to these tools, the proceeding is not level. The party with real-time AI assistance has a measurable advantage in recall, in consistency of argument, and in the ability to respond precisely to what was actually said rather than what they remember being said. That advantage compounds for Self-Represented Litigants, who are already managing their own stress, their own legal unfamiliarity, and the cognitive load of speaking for themselves in a formal setting. Adding a real-time AI assistant to one side of that equation, while the other relies on memory, is not a minor disparity. It is the kind of asymmetry the court system is supposed to guard against.

The other direction is access. Courts that provide AI transcription and summarization to all participants regardless of representation status would eliminate the asymmetry entirely. Some remote hearing platforms are beginning to offer automatic transcription as a native feature. Where that capability exists, it should be made available to every party, not just the attorneys who know to ask for it. The wearable AI gap is a barrier only because courts have not yet decided it is their problem to solve. It is.

Chapter 3 Last Tuesday Night

It is 8:45 PM on a Tuesday. Maria is at her kitchen table when she finds the notice tucked into the door frame. The language is dense, the font is small, and the deadline feels like an approaching storm. In the old system, Maria would spend the next three days in a state of paralyzed anxiety. She would try to call a helpdesk on Wednesday morning, only to be put on hold for forty minutes before being told she needs "Form 12-B" from a courthouse that closes before she gets off work.

But in this system, the door to justice does not lock at 5 PM.

Maria takes a photo of the notice with her phone. She does not have to navigate a complex website; she just sends the image to the court's **Virtual Agent** via SMS. Within seconds, the **Document AI** has read the legalese, identified the case number, and extracted the core issue: a dispute over a broken water heater that led to withheld rent.

At 11:15 PM, while her children are asleep, Maria is "talking" to the agent. It speaks to her in her native Spanish, explaining that she has a legal right to a "Repair and Deduct" defense. The system is not just giving her a PDF link; it is asking her questions to build her response. By midnight, an **agentic workflow** has drafted her answer, attached her photos of the broken heater as evidence, and prepared a fee waiver.

The system reaches its limit when Maria asks if she can sue for emotional distress. Recognizing the complexity, the AI does not guess. A **Human-in-the-Loop (HITL)** checkpoint triggers. The system tells her, *"A clerk will review this and message you by 9 AM."*

On the morning of the hearing, Maria receives a notification. **Spatial Navigation** kicks in, providing a map not just to the courthouse, but to the specific parking lot with the lowest fee and the exact hallway leading to Courtroom 4. She walks through the courthouse doors not as a victim of a confusing process, but as a prepared participant in a transparent one.

For Maria, the technology is invisible. She does not see "tokens" or "MCP servers." She sees a system that listened when she was scared, guided her when she was lost, and stood beside her when she finally walked through the door to claim her rights.

User Journey Map: The Digital-to-Physical Bridge

This journey demonstrates how the individual technologies we have discussed (Virtual Agents, Document AI, and Agentic Systems) stack together to create a single, continuous experience.

The Touchpoint Architecture

Stage	**Action**	**AI Capability**
Inquiry	Maria takes a photo of the eviction notice.	**Document AI (OCR)** identifies the legal intent and urgency.
Explanation	Maria asks, "What does this mean for my kids?"	**Virtual Agent** provides empathetic, plain-language guidance in her native language.
Preparation	The system gathers her evidence (photos/receipts).	**Agentic Reasoning** determines which forms are required based on the facts.

Stage	Action	AI Capability
Drafting	The system populates the response and fee waiver.	**Forms Automation (RPA)** prepares the data for the court's legacy system.
Oversight	Maria asks a nuanced question about damages.	**HITL (Human-in-the-Loop)** triggers a handoff to a human clerk for verification.
Filing	The final documents are submitted to the court.	**RPA / MCP Server** executes the filing and confirms the case number.
Navigation	Maria arrives at the courthouse.	**Spatial Intelligence** provides turn-by-turn wayfinding to the specific courtroom door.

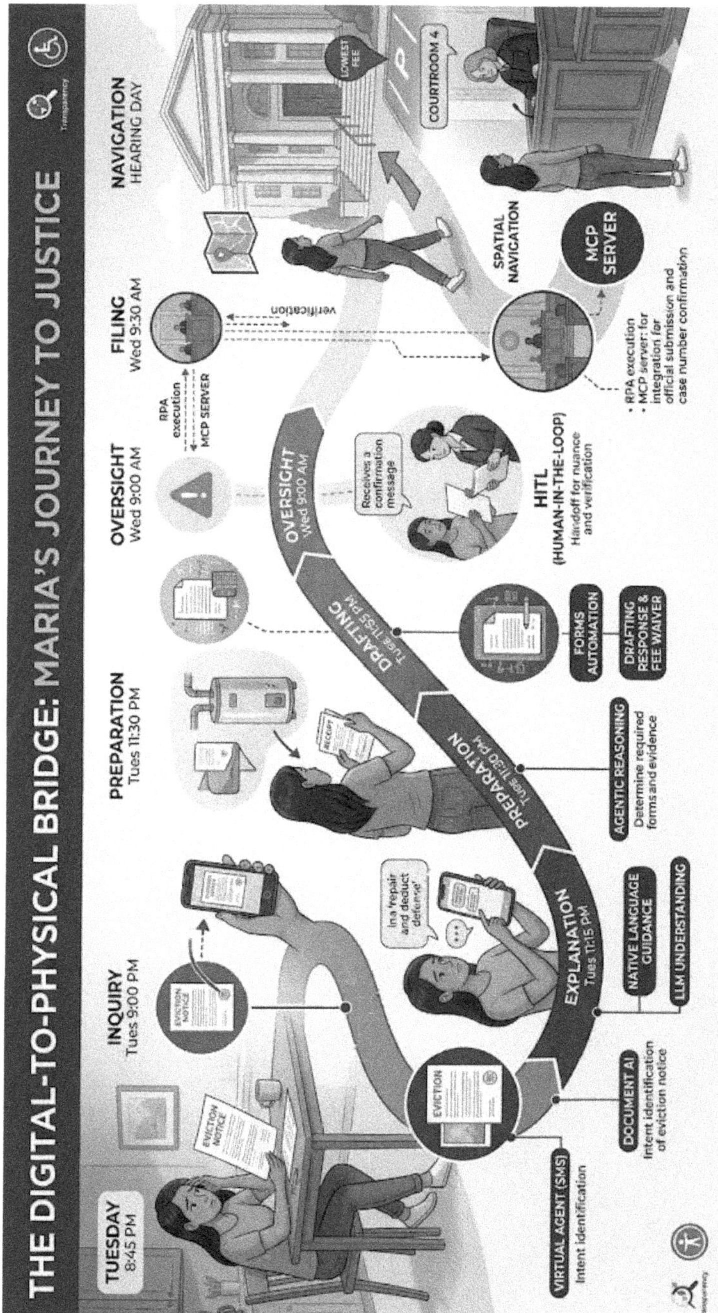

Figure 1: Self-Represented Litigant Journey Map.

Chapter 4 Bridges

Conversational AI

The previous chapter ended with an aspiration: make the technology invisible. This chapter is about the technology that makes that possible. But before the definitions, the architecture, and the implementation decisions, it helps to sit with a simple question. What does it actually mean to be heard?

For most of the history of the legal system, being heard required showing up. In person, during business hours, at the right building, with the right forms, in the right language. If any of those conditions failed, you were not heard. You were turned away. Or you never came at all.

Conversational AI changes that. At its core, it is exactly what the name says: AI that can hold a conversation. Not a form. Not a menu. Not a link to a PDF. A conversation, in plain language, on whatever device the citizen already has, at whatever hour they finally have a moment to deal with the thing that is keeping them up at night. The user does not need to know who to call, which department handles what, which form to file, or what the legal jargon means. They can just ask the question the way they would naturally ask it.

That capability is powered by natural language processing, the ability of a computer to understand and interpret human language as it is actually spoken, not as a keyword search expects it to be typed. Generative AI has dramatically expanded what is possible here. Where early systems recognized phrases and returned scripted responses, modern conversational AI understands context, handles ambiguity, follows a thread across a long exchange, and responds in the same plain language the citizen used. You can find it in web chat, SMS, voice assistants like Alexa and Siri, Messenger, and WhatsApp. The technology is already in people's hands. The question is whether the justice system is on the other end of it.

Not all conversational AI is built the same, and the differences matter more than most procurement conversations acknowledge. The term "chatbot" has become almost derogatory in this space, and for good reason. What courts need, and what citizens deserve, is something more capable. Understanding the spectrum from chatbot to agent to agentic system is the foundation for every implementation decision that follows.

Bot vs. Agent vs. Agentic

In the professional AI space, "chatbot" has become synonymous with the "annoying pop-up that cannot actually help," the digital equivalent of a circular phone menu. For those building sophisticated Access to Justice (A2J) tools, it is a term that minimizes the complexity of the work.

Task vs. Interface vs. Autonomy: The Intelligence Hierarchy

To build a high-trust system, we must distinguish between the tools that follow scripts, the tools that discuss information, and the systems that reason toward an outcome.

1. The Chatbot (The Pre-Scripted Interface)

The **Chatbot** is **deterministic**. It is the entry-level automation most users are familiar with (and often frustrated by). It operates on a "closed loop" of predefined rules and keywords.

- **A2J Example:** A pop-up window that asks, *"Are you here for housing or family law?"* If the user types "eviction," it presents a static link to a PDF.
- **The Limitation:** It cannot handle nuance. If a user says, *"My landlord took the front door off the hinges,"* the chatbot may fail because "hinges" is not in its keyword list.

- **The Reputation:** This is why "chatbot" has become a derogatory term: it suggests a system that is rigid, unhelpful, and incapable of true understanding.

2. The Virtual Agent (The Sophisticated Interface)

The **Virtual Agent** is **probabilistic**. Powered by Large Language Models (LLMs), it is designed for deep, natural language interaction. This is the professional standard for conversational AI in the legal space.

- **A2J Example:** A multilingual interface that can empathize with a tenant, understand that "took my door off" constitutes a constructive eviction, and explain the user's rights in plain language.
- **The Value:** It manages **context and intent**. It can ask follow-up questions and remember the user's name and case details throughout a long session.

3. Agentic (The Reasoning System)

Agentic is a **systemic capability**. While the Virtual Agent *talks*, an Agentic system *acts*. It has the power to **plan, use tools (like RPA or MCP), and self-correct** to achieve a legal goal.

- **A2J Example:** You give the system a goal: *"Stop this illegal eviction."* The agentic system reasons that it needs to pull the court docket via **MCP**, analyze the lease using the **Virtual Agent's** logic, and then trigger an **RPA** action to file an emergency stay.
- **The Value:** It transitions from providing *information* to providing *agency*. It does not just tell you what to do; it helps you do it.

Feature	The Chatbot	Virtual Agent	Agentic System
Logic	Keyword/Script (Rigid)	LLM/Context (Fluid)	Goal-Oriented (Reasoning)
User Experience	"I am stuck in a loop."	"It understands me."	"It is solving my problem."
Implementer Focus	Scripting "If/Then"	Prompt Engineering/RAG	Orchestration/Guardrails
Reliability	High (for simple tasks)	Medium (Hallucination risk)	High (with proper HITL)

For Leaders: Understand that moving from a **Chatbot** to a **Virtual Agent** is a leap in empathy and accessibility. Moving to an a**gentic system** is a leap in power.

For Implementers: Your job is to retire the "Chatbot" and build **Virtual Agents** that serve as the interface for **agentic workflows**. The goal is not "conversation"; the goal is a resolved case.

We are moving from the era of the **chatbot**, which merely deflected queries, to the era of the **Virtual Agent**, which provides guidance, and finally to **agentic systems**, which provide the "Digital Advocate" the public deserves.

Our Implementation of Conversational AI

During my time at the Maricopa County Clerk of the Superior Court, we deployed an IBM Watson-powered conversational AI named Cleo. So named for **CLE**rk **O**f the Superior Court.

Cleo represents a gray area in mid-evolution, where she was more than a chatbot but not quite an agent, as they did not yet exist. We called her an **'assistant'** because of her advanced integrations and capabilities.

We began building Cleo in March of 2019 with an eye on reducing incoming IVR call volumes. While she was structurally ready in June of 2019, we did not launch until the lockdowns were beginning nationwide in March of 2020. This allowed us time to add in a human handoff and expand her subject expertise.

We thought Cleo would reduce call volume. Instead, she revealed a population that had never reached out at all. We did not reduce communication; we expanded it by reaching people who had never engaged with us before.

Cleo was a traditional, dialog-based assistant in which questions elicited predetermined answers, a time before generative AI.

If she was unable to assist in select channels, a human could take over the conversation, review the user's inputs so they did not have to start over, and help resolve their inquiry.

She was able to access our lobby wait management system to tell which locations were busier than others or how many counters were open.

We combined that capability so that when citizens asked for a location, she could identify nearby locations or shorter wait times and proactively offer them.

Channels

What we call "channels" are really doorways to justice. The more doors you create, the more people can walk in. Channels meet people where they already are. Historically, justice systems expect people to come to them. Multi-channel AI inverts that entirely: it brings the system into the citizen's everyday life and expands access hours beyond the 5 PM courthouse close. Channels collapse distance instantly.

Growing up an hour from the courthouse, that distance was not just an inconvenience; it was a message: 'This system is not for you.' With texting capability, a courthouse is in your pocket. Web chat, SMS, Facebook Messenger, WhatsApp, and voice assistants are bridges that knock down barriers people have struggled with for years: geography, transportation, and time. Multi-channel AI gives them a way to ask for help without fear, without sensory overload, without judgment, and at a pace that fits how their minds process the world.

Channels reduce fear, intimidation, and literacy barriers. Some people will not walk into a courthouse because it feels like stepping into enemy territory. A chat window does not judge you. Typing a chat message is familiar. Assistants let people ask questions privately without being judged, breaking down fear of authority, stigma, and anxiety in a way a front counter never can. Text channels (SMS, web chat, Messenger, even email) let people communicate at their own pace. No one is waiting on the other end, no one is judging tone, speed, or hesitation. People can think, re-read, and correct themselves. For people with autism, ADHD, anxiety, or PTSD, this is everything.

Voice assistants remove reading comprehension pressure. Some folks process spoken language better than written. Some process written better than spoken. Channels let them pick the mode that matches their brain's wiring. AI does not judge tone, affect, or eye contact. Humans unconsciously judge monotone voices, "weird" pauses, lack of facial expression, rambling, flat affect, or disorganized storytelling.

AI does not care. This is liberating for neurodiverse users who often fear being misunderstood or dismissed in traditional settings.

Channels also provide sensory-safe environments. Courthouses are overwhelming, even for me: fluorescent lights, noise, crowds, time pressure, security checkpoints. Someone with sensory sensitivity might shut down before they reach the front door. A chatbot is a sensory-neutral doorway. Channels accommodate disabilities in concrete ways, too: screen readers work well with web chat, voice assistants serve the visually impaired, SMS works where hearing or speech is limited, and phones with automated text-back serve as a memory aid for cognitive impairments.

For some, taking time off work to come in is itself a significant barrier. Working parents, shift workers, and caregivers often cannot get help during business hours, but multi-channel AI is available 24/7. The messaging apps they already use, the smart speakers already sitting in their homes, their phone, and their text inbox all remove technological friction and unfamiliar systems. There is a surprising truth in justice tech: people will ask a bot questions they are embarrassed to ask a person. That means more citizens actually seek help before their problems turn into crises, removing shame, fear of sounding uninformed, and fear of retaliation.

Multi-channel conversational AI increases Access to Justice by turning one difficult, intimidating, physical doorway into many familiar, friendly, always-open doorways that meet people where they are, in the format they can actually use. Multiple formats mean there is no single point of exclusion.

Cleo was available on web chat, SMS/text via short or long code, Amazon Alexa, Google Assistant, Facebook Messenger, email, and finally, voice calls.

For the voice channel, we created a hybrid channel experience. We would prompt the user for mobile verification and send them texts with their answers rather than having them write them down or repeat things.

"I see you are calling from number… Rather than writing anything down, would it be okay to send you texts with your answers?"

"No need to write this down, I have sent you a text with this information, but the answer to your question is…."

Chapter 5 Consistency is Fairness

Answers from Data

A carefully curated knowledge layer, updated and reviewed by subject-matter experts, can serve as the single source of truth to deliver uniform answers. That means a clerk in Phoenix, a chatbot in Mesa, or a kiosk in a rural county library all provide the same information: no variation, no "depends on who you talk to." Fairness often begins with consistency. When everyone gets the same answer, everyone stands on equal footing before the law, and trust grows.

Knowledge Base Consistency

Establishing **knowledge base consistency** is the bridge between a promising technical tool and a legally defensible system. In the context of Access to Justice (A2J), consistency is not just a technical requirement—it is a prerequisite for **procedural fairness**. If two individuals with identical legal circumstances receive different guidance because the AI accessed different versions of the "truth," the system has failed the fundamental test of equity.

1. The Architecture of Governance

To build high trust, the knowledge base must move away from "black box" updates toward a **transparent governance framework**.

- **Ownership and Stewardship:** Governance should be led by a **tripartite committee** comprising legal domain experts (judges/attorneys), technologists, and community advocates. This ensures that the "logic" of the AI reflects both current law and the practical realities of the people it serves.
- **The Single Source of Truth (SSOT):** Fairness requires that every AI instance draw from a centralized, immutable-in-transit repository. This prevents "drift" where different regional deployments start providing divergent advice.

2. Dynamic Updates and Versioning

The law is not static; it is a living entity. Managing how an AI "forgets" old law and "learns" new law is critical for implementers.

Automated vs. Human-in-the-Loop Updates

- **Trigger Events:** Updates should be triggered by legislative sessions, landmark court rulings, or scheduled quarterly reviews.
- **The "Sunset" Protocol:** When a statute is repealed, the governance process must include a hard "sunset" date where the old data is archived (for historical reference) and replaced across all nodes simultaneously.

Resolving Version Conflicts

When the law changes, "versioning" becomes a matter of justice. A system must be able to handle **temporal logic**:

- **Date-Stamping:** The AI must evaluate queries based on the date of the incident, not just the current date. For example, a housing dispute from 2024 must be analyzed using 2024 laws, even if the AI is queried in 2026.

This matters more than it might first appear. A tenant who was evicted under a moratorium that has since expired needs the system to know what the law said on the day of their eviction, not what it says today. A person seeking to expunge a conviction needs the system to apply the eligibility criteria that existed at the time of sentencing, which may have been more or less favorable than current law. Getting the temporal logic wrong doesn't produce a minor technical error. It produces a wrong answer delivered with complete confidence to someone who may act on it. Date-stamping is not a nice-to-have feature of a mature system. It is a prerequisite for any system handling matters where the law's relationship to time is part of the question.

- **Conflict Resolution:** If a higher court overrules a lower court during a pending update, the governance layer must have a "Precedence Override" that allows administrators to manually flag certain data points as "Deprecated" or "Superseded" instantly.

3. Auditing for Fairness

An audit is not just a bug check; it is a **justice verification process**.

Audit Type	Frequency	Focus Area
Integrity Audit	Monthly	Ensuring no data corruption or unauthorized "hallucinations" have entered the RAG (Retrieval-Augmented Generation) pipeline.
Bias Audit	Quarterly	Testing if the knowledge base responds differently to identical legal problems when demographic variables (e.g., zip code, language) change.
Legal Accuracy Audit	Post-Legislative Session	Blind testing by legal experts to ensure the AI's "advice" aligns with new statutes.

4. The "Consistency = Fairness" Formula

For leaders and implementers, the value proposition is simple: when the information is uniform, the outcome stops depending on who you talked to or when.

The Fairness Standard: In a consistent system, the quality of justice a user receives is determined by the merits of their case and the law, not by the timing of their query or the specific server their request hit.

When you govern the knowledge base this way, you are not just running cleaner software. You are making a promise to every citizen that the information they get is the same information anyone else would get.

Fairness

In the legal world, "discretion" is often celebrated, but in the context of Access to Justice, it can be a mask for **structural inconsistency**. When the same legal question yields different answers depending on which courthouse clerk answers the phone or which portal a user logs into, the system is not just inefficient—it is fundamentally unfair.

1. The "Wrong Door" Tax

The core equity argument for AI consistency is the elimination of the **"Wrong Door" Tax**. In fragmented legacy systems, a user's success is often tied to their "legal literacy" or sheer luck of the draw.

- **The Lottery of Expertise:** If Clerk A understands the nuances of an eviction moratorium but Clerk B does not, two tenants in identical distress will face opposite outcomes.
- **The Two-Tiered Reality:** Those with resources can hire advocates to knock on every door until they find the "right" answer. Self-Represented Litigants (SRLs) usually only have the energy or data access to knock on one.

2. Consistency as a Civil Right

When we talk about "Structural Fairness," we are arguing that **predictability is a component of due process**.

- **Uniformity is Equity:** Consistency ensures that the law is applied based on the *merits* of the case, not the *medium* of the delivery. A high-governance knowledge base acts as a "Great Leveler," providing a high-quality baseline of information that does not fluctuate based on staff turnover, mood, or unconscious bias.
- **Neutralizing the "Human Variable":** While human empathy is vital, human variability in technical legal interpretation is a liability. A consistent knowledge base ensures that a user in a rural district gets the exact same updated legal guidance as someone in a major tech hub.

3. The Stakeholder "Why"

For Leaders: The Trust Dividend

For leaders, a consistent, audited knowledge base is your protection when something goes wrong. And something will go wrong.

- **Defensibility:** If an agency is sued for providing "bad advice," a consistent, audited knowledge base provides a paper trail of intent and accuracy.
- **Public Trust:** Trust is built on the expectation that the system is "fair" because it is stable. If the AI "changes its mind" every week without a change in law, trust evaporates.

For Implementers: Governance as Mission, Not Chore

If you are building the system, here is the reframe: data governance is not maintenance work. It is the difference between a system that serves everyone equally and one that quietly fails the people who can least afford it.

- **Non-Optionality:** Governance is not a "feature" to be added later; it is the infrastructure of fairness. An ungoverned knowledge base is effectively a machine for generating disparate impact.
- **The "Silent Failure" Risk:** Without structural consistency, the system may fail some users while succeeding for others, making the failure invisible to those at the top while being devastating for the person at the "wrong door."

We do not achieve justice by giving everyone an *answer*; we achieve it by giving everyone the *same right answer.*

Think about the clerk in Phoenix and the chatbot in Mesa from the opening of this chapter. They serve the same county, under the same laws, on the same day. If they give different answers to the same question, one of the citizens who asked leaves better prepared than the other. Not because they had better facts. Not because the law favored them. Because they happened to reach the right door. A well-governed knowledge base closes that gap. It does not guarantee justice. Nothing in this book does. But it removes one of the most persistent and invisible reasons that two identical situations produce different outcomes. That is not a small thing. For the person who would have reached the wrong door, it is everything.

Chapter 6 Finding People (Spatial Access)

Spatial Intelligence

The concept of **Spatial Intelligence** serves as the physical counterpart to the structural fairness we discussed earlier. While structural fairness ensures the "what" of the law is consistent, spatial intelligence ensures the "where" and "how" of accessing that justice are navigable.

In an A2J context, spatial intelligence is not just about robots moving through rooms; it is about an AI's ability to understand the **physicality of the legal system**—the labyrinth of courthouses, the geography of jurisdictions, and the literal distance between a person in crisis and their rights.

I was inspired by a chance run-in with a gentleman while exiting our building one day. I was on a break, heading to the nearby store to get my third Monster of the morning. (Yeah, I know.) Upon reaching the main doors, there was a gentleman gathering his belongings and speaking with the security folks at the checkpoint. He had rushed there, panicked, gone through the security screening, and finally asked where Courtroom B was, only to learn there was no Courtroom B in this building. You could empathically feel the drop in his stomach.

He asked for my help, which I gladly gave. I reviewed the paper he carried and noted that he needed to be a few blocks away. I walked him to the curb, where we could see up the street, and pointed to a tall building on the left. I explained how to navigate the courtyard and find the entrance. He thanked me and hurried on his way.

I resumed walking to the nearby store for more caffeine. As I reached the next intersection, I saw him across the street from me, looking at his paperwork and looking around, uncertain of where he was. He noticed me, and you could see the hope rise in his face. Clearly seeing his plight, I pointed and shouted, "That way," motioning again to the tall building around the corner. Again, he hurried off, and that was the last I saw of him. I do not know what his purpose was that day, but I hope I was able to do something meaningful for him.

1. Defining Spatial Intelligence in A2J

Spatial intelligence is the ability to perceive, reason about, and navigate the physical world. In Access to Justice, it operates through two lenses:

- **The Geographic Lens:** Understanding jurisdictional boundaries. If an AI does not understand that a tenant is fifty feet across a county line, it may provide "consistent" but "locally wrong" advice.
- **The Navigational Lens:** Bridging the gap between digital information and physical action. It is the difference between an AI saying "File this at the courthouse" and an AI saying "The courthouse is two miles away, the accessible entrance is on the north side, and the self-help center is in Room 302."

2. Why Spatial Intelligence is a Fairness Requirement

Without spatial intelligence, AI-driven justice remains abstract. It creates a new "digital-to-physical" gap.

- **The "Last Mile" of Justice:** Many legal failures happen because a user could not physically find the right window or arrive before the door locked. AI with spatial intelligence can provide "procedural wayfinding," turning complex blueprints and transit schedules into actionable guidance.
- **Hyper-Local Fairness:** Justice is often tied to specific geography (e.g., local rent control ordinances). A spatially aware AI recognizes that "fairness" in District A might involve different procedures than District B, even if the state law is the same.
- **Accessibility for the Disabled:** Spatial intelligence allows AI to reason about physical barriers. For a user in a wheelchair, a

"consistent" answer that directs them to a floor with a broken elevator is a denial of justice.

3. The Stakeholder Perspective

For Leaders: Reducing Administrative Friction

For leaders, spatial AI is about reducing friction at every physical touchpoint.

- **Traffic and Wait Times:** By understanding the physical layout and flow of courthouse traffic, AI can direct users to less-busy locations or "digital kiosks" positioned strategically in the community.
- **Evidence Integrity:** In cases involving physical scenes (accidents, property disputes), spatial AI can help users capture "spatially accurate" evidence (e.g., photos with depth and orientation) that is more likely to be admissible.

For Implementers: Grounding the Model

For the technical team, spatial intelligence is about moving beyond **text-only RAG (Retrieval-Augmented Generation)**.

- **Multi-Modal Grounding:** Implementers must integrate GIS (Geographic Information Systems) and BIM (Building Information Modeling) into the knowledge base. The AI needs to "know" the map, not just the manual.
- **Geospatial Guardrails:** Implementation must include "geofencing" logic, ensuring the AI triggers specific warnings or procedural shifts the moment a user's physical location or property address changes the applicable law.

A system that knows the law but does not know the world is only halfway to justice. True access requires an AI that can walk the user from the digital screen to the courtroom door.

Outdoor Spatial Intelligence

Maricopa County is larger than several U.S. states, including Connecticut, Delaware, and Rhode Island combined. The Phoenix-Mesa-Chandler Metropolitan Statistical Area is over 14,000 square miles.

Because of our wide urban sprawl, Cleo had more than knowledge capabilities. One of her abilities was spatial awareness using Esri's ArcGIS technologies, enabling users to find the nearest filing location or obtain turn-by-turn directions. We have multiple filing locations and court facilities.

In a time before context was reasoned by agents, we incorporated an integration with our lobby wait management system to understand how busy a given location was. Users were not just given directions to a location because they asked.

When a user mistook our central downtown location as the place they had to go and requested guidance there, Cleo would provide their answer. She would also recognize that there were locations closer to the citizen or shorter wait times at alternative locations and provide them as options.

Indoor Spatial Intelligence

We provide directions to a location, but we also need to direct THROUGH a location. Like global positioning systems (GPS) guide users outdoors, Indoor Positioning Systems (IPS) bring the familiar "you are here" functionality inside of buildings, displaying the user's real-time position as a blue circle on digital maps. It is often called "blue dot" navigation. It uses a network of Bluetooth Low Energy beacons (BLE) or Wi-Fi to locate devices. It offers immediate, accurate positioning, even showing which floor the user is on.

Figure 2 Example: Blue Dot Application on a Mobile Device.

These technologies were available commercially when Cleo was first created, but were very new and cost-prohibitive to implement the infrastructure and software.

Today, there are newer infrastructure-free solutions that do not require any hardware installations. They are called geomagnetic and use magnetic sensor data from smartphones to display a device's current position on a map.

It is easy for us to forget our comforts in life. Some individuals may not be able to leave work when they need to, and they may need to know exactly how long it will take to complete a transaction with us because the dollars they put in the parking meter are precious to them.

Chapter 7 The Technology and Its Limits

Before this chapter makes the case for caution, it has to build the foundation for it. You cannot weigh a risk you do not understand, and you cannot govern a technology you have only heard described in headlines. The first half of this chapter explains what generative AI actually is, how it has matured into agentic systems, and what it is genuinely capable of in a court setting. The second half examines where it breaks—and why those breaks carry a cost in justice that they do not carry anywhere else.

Generative

Generative AI is a technology that does not just analyze data—it creates. While traditional AI is like a librarian who can find any book in a building, generative AI is like the author who can write a new one based on everything they have ever read. Below is a breakdown of the concept, ranging from a simple analogy to the technical "engine" that powers it.

Imagine an apprentice who spends years watching a master chef. The apprentice does not just memorize recipes; they learn the *essence* of flavor. They notice that a pinch of salt enhances chocolate and that searing meat at high temperatures locks in juices.

Eventually, if you ask this apprentice to "make a dessert that feels like a summer sunset," they do not look up a recipe. Instead, they use their deep understanding of patterns to invent a brand-new dish, perhaps a peach flambé with a blood-orange reduction.

Generative AI is that apprentice. It has "watched" nearly every piece of text, art, or code ever uploaded to the internet, and it uses those patterns to cook up something original.

At its core, generative AI is a prediction engine.

When you ask a text-based AI (like a Large Language Model) a question, it is not "thinking" in the human sense. It is looking at the words you typed and asking itself: "Based on everything I have seen, what is the most statistically likely word to come next?" It does this word by word (or "token" by "token") until it finishes a thought. For images, it works similarly: it starts with a field of "noise" (like static on a TV) and gradually reshapes those pixels until they match the patterns of the object you requested, such as a "golden retriever in a spacesuit."

The breakthrough that made modern generative AI possible is called the **Transformer**. Before Transformers, AI read sentences like a person: one word at a time, left to right. This meant it often forgot the beginning of a long sentence by the time it reached the end.

Technical:

Transformers introduced three key technical concepts:

1. **Self-Attention:** This allows the model to look at *every* word in a sentence simultaneously. In the sentence *"The animal did not cross the street because it was too tired,"* the "Self-Attention" mechanism helps the AI realize that "it" refers to the "animal." In a different sentence, *"The animal did not cross the street because it was too wide,"* it realizes "it" refers to the "street."
2. **Embeddings:** The AI converts words into numbers and plots them in a massive, multi-dimensional map. Words with similar meanings (like "dog" and "puppy") are mathematically "near" each other in this space.
3. **Parameters:** Think of these as the "knobs and dials" inside the AI's brain. When we say a model has 175 billion parameters, we mean it has 175 billion tiny settings that it adjusted during training to get better at predicting the next word.

Why 2026 is Different

In the early days, generative AI was a "chatbot." By 2026, it has evolved into **agentic AI**.

- **Multimodality:** Modern models do not just "read." They can "see" a photo of your broken sink and "write" a repair guide simultaneously.
- **Reasoning vs. Regurgitation:** We are moving past the AI simply repeating facts. New architectures allow the AI to "think" before it speaks, checking its own logic and correcting errors before you ever see the output.
- **Action-Oriented:** AI is not just generating a draft of an email anymore; it is logging into your calendar, finding a time that works for everyone, and sending the invite autonomously.

Generative AI represents a shift from human-driven creation to human-directed creation. We are no longer the ones swinging the hammer; we are the architects providing the blueprints, while the AI does the heavy lifting of building the structure.

Potential Use Cases

Before we go deeper into how the technology works and where it breaks, it helps to see the landscape of how courts are actually using it. There are two broad categories. AI that helps staff do their jobs better, and AI that helps citizens navigate the system without staff having to be in the room. Both matter. Both carry risk. And both are already happening in courts across the country.

The most visible use is the virtual assistant. A citizen goes to the court website at 10 PM because they just got served and they are scared, and there is something there that can actually help them. It answers "how do I file?" and "what forms do I need?" and "what does this legal term mean?" without requiring a lawyer, without requiring a clerk, without requiring business hours. That is not a small thing. That is the gate opening for someone who would otherwise have gone to bed more afraid than they started. Cleo, the Watson-powered assistant we built at the Maricopa County Clerk of the Superior Court, was exactly this. She did not replace our staff. She reached people who had never reached us at all.

Document AI is the back-office counterpart. Courts process enormous volumes of paper every day: pleadings, motions, affidavits, intake forms. AI can classify those documents, extract the relevant data, catch missing fields before a clerk ever touches the file, and route everything to the right workflow. Chapter 8 goes deep on this. What matters here is the access argument: when a citizen's filing gets rejected because of a missing field they did not know was required, that is not just an administrative inconvenience. It is a delay in an eviction case, a custody matter, or an order of protection. Document AI catches those errors before they become setbacks.

Scheduling and docket management are areas courts are beginning to explore carefully. AI can analyze historical data to predict no-show rates, identify conflicts before they cascade, and help administrators allocate courtroom resources more effectively. I treat this category with more caution than the others. The closer AI gets to the actual movement of cases, the more important human oversight becomes. These are productivity tools for administrators, not decision-makers for outcomes.

Legal research and knowledge retrieval are where AI is already transforming the daily work of clerks, attorneys, and judges. Tools like Westlaw CoCounsel, Harvey, and Lexis+ AI allow legal professionals to ask natural language questions across vast repositories of statutes, case law, and procedural rules and get summarized, sourced results in seconds. "What are the filing requirements for an eviction case?" "Show recent rulings on digital evidence admissibility." A task that once took hours of manual searching now takes minutes. This does not replace legal judgment; it clears the retrieval work that precedes it so judgment has room to operate. There is an important distinction courts must hold onto, however. These tools are built for trained legal professionals who can evaluate the output, recognize when a citation has been overruled, and distinguish between controlling and persuasive authority. A Self-Represented Litigant using the same tool unsupervised is not in the same position. The power of the tool does not change based on who is holding it. The risk does. Chapter 9 addresses this distinction directly.

Sentiment and trend analysis is one of the quieter use cases, but one of the most useful for leaders. When you review call transcripts, chatbot logs, and complaint submissions through an AI lens, patterns surface that you would not see any other way. Which forms generate the most errors. Which processes produce the most confusion. Where in the journey citizens are most likely to give up. That is not just operational intelligence—it is a map of where the system is failing people. Chapter 9 covers this directly.

Risk monitoring and compliance is the category courts approach most carefully, and rightly so. AI can flag when required notices were not sent, when deadlines were missed, and when documents failed validation. That is genuinely useful. But courts must be disciplined about the line between AI that monitors compliance and AI that makes compliance determinations. Systems that influence sentencing, bail, or legal outcomes require a level of governance, transparency, and human oversight that most organizations are not yet ready for. The guiding principle has not changed from Chapter 1: AI is a guide, not a decider.

Vibe coding is emerging as both a force multiplier and a cautionary tale. At its best, it allows a seasoned developer to describe a system in plain language and have AI generate working code in seconds, compressing weeks of work into hours. For a court technology team with limited resources trying to build a forms automation workflow or a document-routing bot, that kind of acceleration is real and meaningful. But vibe coding is only as good as the judgment of the person directing it. An experienced developer knows when the generated code is brittle, when the logic is subtly wrong, and when the security assumptions are dangerous. A new developer may not. They see code that runs and assume code that works. In a justice context, those are not the same thing. A vibe-coded bot that processes eviction filings incorrectly does not just fail a unit test. It fails a person. Used by the right hands, vibe coding is one of the most powerful tools available to under-resourced public-sector teams. Used carelessly, it ships confidence without competence. Courts adopting it need to be honest about what they have.

Virtual humans are a use case courts should be watching closely. These are photorealistic AI-animated figures that can be deployed on a mobile screen, a lobby kiosk, or a self-help terminal, and they change the access equation in ways a text chatbot cannot. For neurodiverse citizens, the ability to choose the appearance of the person they are interacting with matters more than most technologists recognize. Someone who has difficulty speaking to people of a particular gender, or who freezes in front of certain physical presentations, may find a virtual human they select themselves far easier to approach than a clerk they cannot control. These systems are also beginning to understand body language and facial expression. When you smile, they smile. When your expression drops, they register that. A well-designed virtual human knows that the person requesting a death certificate is not in the same emotional space as someone asking about a parking ticket, and it should respond accordingly. Some virtual humans are beginning to interpret and respond in ASL. The accessibility implications of that alone are significant. The caution here is the same as in every other part of this book: the technology must serve the person, not impress the administrator. A virtual human that smiles through a grief-stricken request because no one configured it for emotional context is not more accessible. It is more alienating. Get the design right.

AI in the hearing room is a use case courts cannot afford to treat as someone else's problem. AI note takers, wearable recording devices, and ambient transcription tools are already present in courtrooms and virtual hearings, mostly invisibly, mostly without policy. The fairness and recording restriction dimensions of this are addressed in Chapter 2, but the use case belongs here as well: courts have an opportunity to deploy hearing room AI affirmatively, as a tool for all parties rather than an advantage for the few. Automatic transcription of all proceedings, made available to every participant in real time regardless of representation status, would eliminate the asymmetry that currently exists while also producing better records. Courts that wait for parties to raise objections before developing a policy are already behind.

Evidence integrity is an emerging use case courts need to get ahead of rather than react to. Generative AI has made it possible to produce convincing synthetic photographs, video, and audio with consumer-grade tools. At the same time, a set of detection technologies and a content provenance standard called C2PA are beginning to offer courts tools to verify the authenticity of evidence. Neither the threat nor the solution is hypothetical. Both are already present in proceedings. The fuller treatment of evidence integrity, including what the detection tools can and cannot do, the C2PA standard, and the fairness implications for litigants who cannot afford forensic expertise, is in Chapter 7.

None of these use cases works in isolation, and none of them is free of risk. The rest of this chapter is about understanding the technology well enough to deploy it responsibly. The use cases above are the "what." What follows is the "how" and the "what can go wrong." Both matter equally.

Translation

For decades, digital translation was a mechanical process of substitution, a digital dictionary swapping a word in one language for its closest equivalent in another. It was functional, but brittle. It stumbled on idioms, ignored cultural nuances, and often stripped away the speaker's original intent.

With the advent of **Generative AI**, translation has undergone a fundamental metamorphosis. We have moved from **Translation** (word-matching) to **Localization** (context-matching). Modern Large Language Models (LLMs) do not just see words; they understand the "latent space" where concepts live. When a citizen speaks in Spanish, Navajo, Tagalog, or American Sign Language (ASL), the system is not just looking for a bridge between two dictionaries. It is interpreting the cultural weight, the emotional tone, and the situational context of the request.

The Death of the "Exclusionary Second"

In public service, time is often the silent gatekeeper. We have long accepted a world where non-English speakers must wait for an interpreter to be scheduled, or endure the awkward, staggered silence of a three-way phone call.

In these moments, the delay is not just an inconvenience—it is a barrier to equity. As the saying goes: **"Every second a citizen spends waiting for translation is a second of exclusion."** By integrating real-time speech-to-text and low-latency text-to-speech, we eliminate that gap. The system responds fluently and instantly. This creates a "consistency of fairness" where the quality of service a person receives is no longer tethered to the language they speak at home.

Accessibility as Justice

This technological leap is reshaping the very definition of accessibility:

- **Hyper-Local Inclusion:** Generative AI allows us to support indigenous languages like Navajo or low-resource dialects that were previously ignored by commercial software.

- **Visual-to-Vocal:** For the Deaf community, computer vision can now translate ASL into spoken English in real time, while simultaneously turning spoken responses back into a visual avatar that signs.
- **The Dignity of the Direct Voice:** Perhaps most importantly, it grants citizens the dignity of a direct connection. They are no longer a "case file" waiting for an intermediary; they are participants in their own government.

Language access is not a luxury or a modern convenience. It is **justice access**. When we remove the language barrier, we are not just helping people understand; we are ensuring they are heard.

Technical:

Neural Machine Translation (NMT) vs. LLMs: Traditional translation used NMT, which focused on sequences of words. Generative AI uses **High-Dimensional Embeddings**. Imagine every concept (like "justice") as a point in a 3D map. Generative AI finds the exact point for that concept in English and its equivalent "geographic" point in Tagalog, ensuring the *idea* is preserved, even if the grammatical structure is entirely different.

LMs, Agentic, and Reasoning

To understand the modern AI landscape in 2026, it helps to view these three concepts not as different "types" of AI, but as different **levels of maturity** in how a digital brain functions.

Here is a breakdown of Language Models, Reasoning, and Agency, demystified through the analogy of a **Travel Professional.**

1. Language Models (LMs): The "Library of Alexandria"

At the foundational level, we have the Language Model. This is the "brain" that has read everything.

- **The Concept:** An LM is a statistical map of human knowledge. It understands how words relate to each other, the tone of a legal document versus a fairy tale, and the grammar of nearly every language.
- **The Analogy:** Imagine a **Travel Researcher** who has read every guidebook, blog, and brochure ever written. If you ask them, "What is a good hotel in Paris?" they can instantly describe five options based on what they have read.
- **The Limitation:** They are "reactive." They do not *do* anything until you ask, and they do not double-check if that hotel in Paris closed down yesterday. They are simply sharing what they "know."

2. Reasoning: The "Deliberate Thinker"

Reasoning is a layer of **deliberation** added to the Language Model. In earlier years, AI would "blurp" out an answer instantly. Today's reasoning models "think" before they speak.

- **The Concept:** Using a process called "Chain of Thought" or "Inference-Time Compute," the AI creates an internal monologue. It breaks a complex problem into smaller logical steps, checks its own work for contradictions, and discards bad ideas before presenting the final answer to you.
- **The Analogy:** Now, our Travel Researcher becomes a **Travel Consultant**. When you ask for a hotel, they do not just list them. They think: *"The user has a toddler, so they need an elevator. It is July, so air conditioning is a must. Hotel A is great, but too far from the metro."* They deliberate internally to provide a logically sound recommendation.
- **The Signifier:** You will often see a "Thinking..." bubble or a "Reasoning" status. It is slower than a standard LM, but much more accurate.

3. Agentic AI: The "Autonomous Executor"

Agentic AI is the move from **knowing** and **thinking** to **doing**. An "agent" has a goal, a set of tools (like a web browser, a credit card, or a calendar), and the authority to use them.

- **The Concept:** Agentic systems operate in a loop: **Perceive → Reason → Act → Observe.** They do not just give you a plan; they execute it. If an agent hits a roadblock (e.g., a website is down), it does not stop and ask you what to do; it "re-reasons" and finds a different way to achieve the goal.
- **The Analogy:** This is a **Full-Service Travel Agent**. You do not just get a list of hotels. You say, "Book me a trip to Paris under $3,000," and the Agent:
    1. Searches live flight data (Action).
    2. Realizes the budget is tight (Reasoning).
    3. Finds a deal, logs into your account, and completes the booking (Agency).
- **The Result:** You are not managing a tool; you are managing a **result**.

Summary Table: The Evolution of AI

Feature	Language Model (LM)	Reasoning Model	Agentic AI
Core Strength	Vast Knowledge	Logic & Accuracy	Autonomy & Action
Primary Output	Text/Information	A proven "Chain of Thought"	A completed task
Human Role	Asks a question	Reviews the logic	Sets the goal
Analogy	The Book	The Scholar	The Employee

What to Expect: Accuracy and Performance

One of the most common questions leaders ask before a deployment is some version of "how accurate will it be?" The honest answer is: it depends, and the number matters less than you think. A practical benchmark is 60–80% task success in early deployment, improving to 85–95% with constraints, feedback loops, and domain tuning. But that single number conceals most of what actually matters.

Accuracy for agentic systems is not one number. Unlike a classifier that returns a right or wrong answer, agentic systems operate across multi-step workflows. Accuracy fragments into at least five distinct measures: task success rate (did it complete the goal?), step reliability (did each action execute correctly?), decision quality (did it choose the right path or tool?), content correctness (was the output factually right?), and recovery ability (did it detect and fix its own mistakes?). A system can be 80% accurate at content generation but only 55% successful end-to-end if tool use or branching fails. Measuring only the part that looks good gives you a false sense of readiness.

Every new channel introduces a performance drop. When you deploy into a new channel or serve a new audience, expect degradation. Users do not behave like your training data. Input is less structured. Errors compound: speech-to-text feeds into NLU, which feeds into planning, which feeds into execution, and each layer multiplies the risk. A useful rule of thumb: every new layer or channel introduces a 5–20% performance drop unless explicitly tuned for it. The table below shows realistic ranges across capability areas as a system matures from initial deployment to instrumented production.

Capability	Initial (new environment)	Mature (instrumented + tuned)
Intent understanding	70–85%	90–97%
Tool / API execution	60–80%	85–95%
Multi-step task completion	50–75%	80–95%

Capability	Initial (new environment)	Mature (instrumented + tuned)
Hallucination-free responses	60–85%	90–98%
End-to-end success	50–70%	85–95%

That 50–70% early end-to-end success rate is the number most teams underestimate. It does not mean the system is failing—it means the system is new. The gap between that number and 90%+ is closed not by the model alone, but by the infrastructure around it.

Agentic systems fail differently from traditional software. A traditional system crashes or throws an error. An agentic system fails silently: confidently wrong actions, partial task completion, incorrect tool selection, and degradation that surfaces no error at all. This is why measuring only "accuracy" misses the actual risk. You need observability, trace-level evaluation, and Human-in-the-Loop checkpoints early on. The absence of an error message is not the same as success.

High-performing teams do not rely on the model alone. Systems that reach 90%+ add guardrails and constrained action spaces, deterministic fallbacks, tool validation layers, retrieval grounding (RAG), structured prompts and schemas, user confirmation for critical steps, and continuous evaluation loops running both offline and live. Without these, most systems plateau around 70–80% and stay there. The model is not the ceiling—the architecture is.

Expect regression when you add guardrails. This is one of the most frustrating operational realities of agentic system development, and one of the least discussed. When you add a guardrail to fix a known problem, you will often create a new one. A guardrail that stops hallucinations in one domain begins over-triggering on legitimate questions in a related domain. You tighten knowledge base boundaries to prevent context bleeding, and now the system refuses to answer edge-case questions it handled correctly before. You add a validation layer to catch bad form data, and it starts rejecting valid filings from citizens whose input is non-standard but legally sound. The fix works. Something else breaks.

This is called regression, and in a justice context, it carries a particular danger: the failures it creates are often quieter than the ones it fixes. An over-triggered guardrail does not crash the system. It simply refuses to help someone who needs help. That person may not complain, may not know they failed, and may not try again. Regression in justice AI does not always look like a bug. It can look like silence.

The discipline required is regression testing before every change, not just after something breaks. Every guardrail addition, every knowledge base update, every prompt schema change should be run against a fixed set of test cases that cover both the problem you are solving and the things that were already working. Without that, you are flying blind, improving one metric while quietly degrading others. The cost-weighted framing matters here too: if your regression testing prioritizes high-stakes failure cases, you are far more likely to catch the kind of silent failure that puts someone in the wrong courtroom or sends them home without the filing they needed.

Plan for three phases, not one launch. A production-minded rollout for court and government use cases should expect distinct performance bands across phases rather than a single go-live target.

Phase	Autonomous success	Needs human assist	Failure
Phase 1 (pilot/new audience)	50–70%	20–30%	5–15%
Phase 2 (stabilized)	75–90%	<15%	<5%
Phase 3 (mature, high trust)	90–95%+	<5%	<1–2% critical

Track cost-weighted task success, not raw accuracy. For public-sector applications, raw accuracy is the wrong metric to optimize for. What matters is the cost of failure. Wrong legal guidance carries a high cost: it can affect someone's housing, custody, or freedom. Slightly awkward phrasing carries a low cost. A system that is "92% accurate" but fails on high-stakes edge cases is more dangerous than one at 85% that fails gracefully on low-stakes queries. Instrument your system to track what kind of failures you are having, not just how many.

In a court or constituent services deployment, that means expecting wide variability early, designing for progressive trust (assist before you automate), keeping humans in the loop for edge cases, and instrumenting everything from the start. You will need that data. The teams that reach phase three are not the ones with the best models. They are the ones who built the feedback loop first.

Bias of Misfortune (Hallucinations, Context Bleeding, Context Compression, and Ignored System Prompts & Guardrails)

This section explores how technical glitches in AI are not just "bugs"; they are systemic barriers. When these errors occur in a legal or social services setting, they do not just result in a wrong answer; they result in a denial of rights. These newer technologies come with unpredictable risks. And the stakes are dramatically higher when the subject is justice. If a model fails a person seeking Access to Justice even once, it can create what I call a "bias of misfortune."

It is not demographic. I call it that because it may never repeat. It could be platform-specific. Something that happens to a given technology but not another. It could come from a unique sequence of questions that only one person ever asks.

A single hallucination or leaked context could misinform someone about their rights. It could affect their freedom, their children, their finances, or their livelihood. The same people who already face barriers to justice are the ones who would be harmed the most.

One mistake can change a life.

We cannot allow that. Not for justice. Not even a single time.

Because of that, we made a deliberate choice. Rather than bringing court-specific knowledge into a general-purpose agentic system, we route citizens to a separate, court-specific experience that uses a traditional, deterministic dialog-based assistant.

Not because generative AI or reasoning models are incapable, they absolutely could handle most justice questions. In justice, "almost always correct" is failure.

When designing for safety, the justice system cannot gamble with hallucinations or context bleeding. The stakes are high: liberty, family, finances, shelter, justice. AI must be built with safety woven into its architecture.

Safety means more than filters. You need structured knowledge bases for high-risk topics.

Deterministic responses in sensitive domains.

It means human checkpoints for sensitive moments.

When you use generative solutions, it means isolating domains so information never bleeds between unrelated topics. Generative solutions need clear statements of capability and limitation.

In the world of generative AI, technical errors are often discussed as quirky inconveniences. But in the context of justice, an error is an exclusion. Below are the four horsemen of AI-driven inequity. We cannot afford to "hope" models behave; we must design them to behave.

1. Hallucinations: The Eloquent Lie

A "hallucination" occurs when a model provides a confident, fluent response that is factually false. Because these models are built on probability, they prioritize "sounding right" over "being right."

- **The Impact on Justice:** Imagine a citizen asking an AI about the requirements for an emergency housing voucher. If the AI "hallucinates" a deadline that does not exist or a document that is not required, the citizen may lose their home. In justice, a hallucination is a **fabricated barrier.**

2. Context Bleeding: The Ghost in the Machine

Context bleeding happens when information from one part of a conversation (agentic subagents or a previous training set) "leaks" into another. The AI loses the "clean lines" between two different scenarios.

- **The Impact on Justice:** If a system is processing a high volume of legal aid requests, "bleeding" might cause the AI to apply the facts of a domestic violence case to a simple landlord-tenant dispute. When the AI fails to keep individual lives distinct, it erodes the **due process** of being treated as a unique person with unique circumstances.

3. Context Compression: The Loss of Nuance

To save "memory" (tokens), AI systems often "compress" long conversations. They keep the gist but discard the details. While efficient, this acts like a sieve that catches the big rocks but lets the sand slip through.

- **The Impact on Justice:** The "sand" is where the nuance lives. A citizen's explanation of *why* they missed a court date, perhaps a medical emergency or a lack of transit, can be compressed away by the AI as "irrelevant detail." When we compress context, we **dehumanize the data**, stripping away the very mitigating factors that the justice system is supposed to consider.

4. Ignored System Prompts and Guardrails: The Safety Paradox

System prompts are *instructions given directly to the model* at runtime. They shape how the model behaves in a specific conversation. Think of them as the "role + rules" the model is told to follow.

- Example: "You are a helpful legal assistant. Do not give definitive legal advice."
- They are flexible, editable, and context-specific.

Guardrails are *broader controls around the model*, often enforced outside or alongside the prompt. They are about safety, reliability, and policy compliance.

- Examples:
    - Content moderation filters
    - Input/output validation
    - Tool-use restrictions
    - Rate limits or fallback logic
- They are typically more rigid and harder for end users to override.

Guardrails are the "rules" programmed into AI to prevent it from being biased or harmful. However, these guardrails can be brittle. Sometimes they fail (letting harm through), and other times they are "over-active," refusing to answer perfectly legal and necessary questions out of an abundance of caution.

Key difference:

- System prompt = *guidance inside the model's reasoning*
- Guardrails = *constraints enforced on or around the system*

In practice, good systems use both:

- System prompts to steer behavior
- Guardrails to enforce boundaries when prompts are not enough

The Impact on Justice: This creates a **Safety Tax.** A wealthy person with a lawyer does not need to worry about AI guardrails. But a low-income citizen relying on an AI "legal navigator" might find the system refusing to give advice because the guardrail thinks the topic is "too sensitive." When the AI stays silent to "be safe," the citizen is left in the dark. Ignored or over-applied guardrails become a **denial of service.**

These behaviors are rarely intentional, but their impact is felt most by those already at the margins.

The Consistency Gap: A person with resources can verify an AI's hallucination or push back against a "compressed" summary. A person in crisis, facing a language barrier or a lack of legal literacy, may take the AI's word as absolute truth.

A hallucination is not just a technical fluke. It is a **violation of trust.** Context bleeding is not just a memory error. It is a **blurring of identity.** To build a just system, we must treat these not as "bugs to be patched," but as "inequities to be engineered out of existence."

The Moral Circuit Breaker: Human-in-the-Loop (HITL)

In the architecture of justice, a "Human-in-the-Loop" (HITL) is more than a quality control measure. It is a **moral circuit breaker**. It ensures that while the AI provides the speed, a human provides the soul and the ultimate accountability.

If the technical failures of AI (hallucinations, bleeding, and compression) are the "Bias of Misfortune," then **Human-in-the-Loop (HITL)** is the safeguard of dignity. HITL is the requirement that a human expert remains involved in the AI's decision-making process, reviewing, verifying, or overriding the machine's output before it impacts a person's life.

In a justice-oriented system, HITL transforms the AI from a **judge** into a **clerk**.

1. Verification vs. Velocity

AI provides velocity; humans provide verification. An AI can scan 10,000 pages of legal code in seconds, but it cannot "feel" the weight of a wrongful eviction. By placing a human in the loop, we ensure that an AI's "eloquent lie" (hallucination) is caught before it becomes a legal reality. The human acts as a filter, sifting the AI's speed through the lens of lived experience.

2. Restoring the Lost Nuance

Where **Context Compression** tends to flatten a citizen's story into a sterile summary, a human reviewer can look at the original input and say, *"Wait, the AI missed the fact that the Defendant was in the hospital."* The human "uncompresses" the data, restoring the vital details that make a case a human story rather than a data point.

3. Overriding the "Safety Tax"

When **Ignored Guardrails** cause an AI to shut down or refuse to help a citizen with a sensitive but necessary request, a Human-in-the-Loop can step in. Humans can understand the difference between "harmful content" and a "desperate plea for legal help." The human loop ensures that safety protocols protect the user without paralyzing the service.

4. Accountability: The "Who" in the System

The "Responsibility Gap" is the greatest danger of an autonomous system. If an AI makes a mistake that leads to a denial of justice, you cannot put an algorithm in jail or sue a piece of code. HITL ensures there is a clear line of **human accountability**.

The Golden Rule of Justice AI: No life-altering decision (no denial of benefits, no determination of guilt, no loss of housing) should ever be finalized by an AI alone.

The "Human-Led, AI-Augmented" Spectrum

HITL is not a single checkbox. It is a spectrum of oversight:

- **Human-in-the-loop:** The AI suggests, but the human must click "approve" for every single action.

- **Human-on-the-loop:** The AI performs tasks autonomously, but a human monitors the process in real time and can "intervene" at any second to stop it.
- **Human-out-of-the-loop:** The AI acts entirely alone. (In the context of justice, this is the "Danger Zone.")

Guarding the "Agentic Loop"

In agentic systems, the loop is: **Plan → Act → Observe → Re-plan.** If a human is not part of that cycle, the AI can enter a "death spiral." For example, if an AI agent fails to log into a government site, it might "reason" that it needs to try 1,000 times, inadvertently launching a DDoS attack on a public service portal. HITL ensures a human can "pull the plug" when the AI's autonomous reasoning becomes irrational.

The Bottom Line

By keeping a human in the loop, we acknowledge that **justice is a human endeavor.** We use the AI to clear the paperwork and the language barriers so that the humans can focus on what they do best: exercising judgment, empathy, and fairness.

Language access is justice access, but human oversight is the guarantee that the access remains just.

The Agentic Paradox: Autonomy vs. Accountability

As AI moves from being a "Consultant" (Reasoning) to an "Agent" (Action), the "exclusionary second" we discussed earlier is nearly eliminated. However, it is replaced by a new danger: the **Autonomous Error.**

If an agentic system is tasked with "Helping a citizen clear a wrongful eviction from their record," it does not just provide instructions. It might log into a portal, draft a motion, and file it. If that agent operates under a **Hallucination** or suffers from **Context Bleeding**, it could file incorrect legal documents that permanently damage the citizen's standing.

The "Gatekeeper" Model of HITL

For agentic AI, the human loop must shift from being a "reviewer" to a **Gatekeeper**. This involves two critical structures:

1. **Checkpoint Consent:** The Agent is allowed to do the research, draft the documents, and prepare the filing, but it hits a "hard wall" before any action is taken. It must present its "Chain of Thought" to a human supervisor, explaining *why* it chose this path and *what* the result will be. The action only triggers upon a human signature.
2. **Tool-Use Auditing:** Agents use "tools" (APIs, web browsers, databases). A robust HITL system logs every tool call. If the Agent tries to access a database it should not, or interprets a legal statute incorrectly, the human can see the exact moment the logic failed.

The Ethics of the "Digital Handshake"

We must view the collaboration between human and agentic AI as a **Digital Handshake**. The AI provides the tireless capability to navigate complex bureaucracies, but the human provides the "Moral North Star."

Synthetic Evidence: The Fifth Horseman

The four horsemen described in the Bias of Misfortune section, hallucinations, context bleeding, context compression, and ignored guardrails, all operate inside AI systems that courts deploy. This fifth one operates outside them, in the hands of parties, in the evidence they submit, and in the integrity of the record the court relies on to reach a just outcome. Generative AI has fundamentally changed what a photograph, a video, and an audio recording can prove. Courts have not yet caught up.

The threat is real and accessible. A convincing deepfake video can be produced today by someone with moderate technical skill and a consumer-grade laptop. A synthetically generated photograph, complete with fabricated EXIF metadata and plausible timestamps, is achievable with tools available to anyone willing to spend a few hours learning them. An AI-altered audio recording, where words are added, removed, or reordered, requires even less. The legal standard for authenticating photographic and video evidence, Federal Rule of Evidence 901 in federal courts and its state equivalents, was not written for a world where any visual record might be entirely synthetic. The heuristic of "it looks real" has always done a great deal of authentication work in practice. That heuristic is now broken.

Detection tools exist. They are useful and insufficient at the same time. A growing set of tools, including Reality Defender, Hive Moderation, Sensity AI, and Microsoft's Video Authenticator, use AI models to analyze whether content is likely to have been synthetically generated or manipulated. Some return confidence scores. Some flag specific regions of an image or video frame where artifacts suggest manipulation. These tools are genuinely useful. They are also genuinely probabilistic. A detection model that is 95% accurate sounds reassuring until you consider what it means in a courtroom. At 95% accuracy, five out of every hundred determinations are wrong. In a high-stakes proceeding, that is not a confidence interval. It is a risk to a person's freedom, their children, and their home. Courts that treat detection tool output as definitive are misunderstanding what the tool is telling them. Courts that ignore these tools entirely are not safer. They are just uninformed.

Content provenance is the more durable answer. The Coalition for Content Provenance and Authenticity (C2PA) has developed an open standard for cryptographically signing digital content at the moment of capture. A photograph taken on a C2PA-enabled camera carries a tamper-evident manifest: who captured it, when, where, on what device, and whether it has been subsequently modified. Any alteration after capture breaks the cryptographic signature. This is not AI detecting AI. It is a chain-of-custody standard applied to digital content the same way chain of custody has always been applied to physical evidence. Adobe, Microsoft, Google, Sony, Nikon, and others have committed to the standard. Some devices already ship with C2PA support built in. Courts that begin building familiarity with C2PA now, and that ask about provenance metadata when digital evidence is submitted, will be ahead of the jurisdictions that wait until they have a deepfake problem in front of them.

The fairness argument connects back to the core of this book. Generating convincing synthetic evidence requires resources: technical skill, time, and access to the right tools. Challenging synthetic evidence also requires resources: forensic expertise, detection tools, and the budget to retain an expert witness who can explain the analysis to a judge or jury. A well-resourced party can afford both the generation and the counter-detection. A Self-Represented Litigant can afford neither. The justice gap does not only exist before the courthouse door. It exists inside the evidence itself. A domestic violence survivor whose abuser submits a synthetic video is not in a position to retain a digital forensics expert. A tenant in an eviction proceeding who cannot identify manipulated photographs of the property has no practical recourse if the court lacks the tools or the policy to examine the question. Courts that treat evidence integrity as a technical problem for parties to sort out are abdicating a responsibility that belongs to the institution.

Three things courts can do now, before the policy fully catches up: ask about digital provenance as a standard part of evidence authentication for photographs, video, and audio; develop relationships with digital forensics resources that Self-Represented Litigants can access without cost; and treat detection tool output as a flag for expert review rather than a determination. The technology will continue to improve on both sides of this problem. The institutional response cannot wait for the technology to resolve it.

Chapter 8 Case Initiation (Document AI + Forms + RPA)

Document AI

There are other ways AI can expand Access to Justice. Document AI is powerful, especially in case initiation. You may ask: if humans already initiate cases, why do we need it? Document AI does not replace humans. It removes the barriers that prevent humans from helping as many people as they could. Filing a case is overwhelming for many people: forms are long, legal language is complex, and mistakes are easy. Document AI is more than accepting online form submissions. It can extract information from messy paperwork, classify filings correctly, highlight missing fields, and guide users on what is incomplete. Citizens do not have to understand legal structure or guess at what the court is asking for just to get started. It lowers the barrier to beginning a case, which is often the hardest step, and eliminates rejections and delays caused by avoidable filing errors.

Humans spend enormous time returning filings because of missing sections, wrong case type, incorrect attachments, and illegible handwriting. Document AI catches these errors instantly, before a clerk ever sees the document. That means fewer citizen setbacks, fewer "start over" moments, fewer days lost to re-filing. That alone improves access dramatically. Clerks and intake staff want to help people deeply, but they are often buried under repetitive, mechanical tasks like data entry, scanning, categorizing, routing documents, and verifying completeness. Document AI takes that load off their plate, freeing staff to do the work only humans can do: explaining processes, calming anxious litigants, resolving confusion, helping people who truly need human intervention. AI gives staff more time to be human, not less.

Document AI also protects people with low literacy, language barriers, disabilities, or neurodivergence. Some citizens struggle to fill out forms accurately because of reading comprehension, legal jargon, dyslexia, ADHD, language limitations, or cognitive overload. Document AI does not judge them for it. It quietly interprets their forms, extracts needed data, and ensures nothing is missed, compensating for the same systemic barriers that shut people out long before they reach a clerk. It also enables case initiation across multiple channels. Without it, filing must happen in person during business hours with a clerk present. With Document AI, filings can come from mobile apps, kiosks, online uploads, partner agencies, or community centers. The citizen no longer needs to physically travel, take time off work, or wait in line. For rural populations like the one I grew up with, that matters.

Document AI creates consistency and fairness, which are bedrock principles of trust in any justice system. Some courts and clerks are not permitted to provide legal advice, even advice related to forms, and different staff interpret documents slightly differently; that is human nature. Document AI ensures consistent classification, consistent routing, consistent validation, and consistent extraction. Consistency is not just efficient, it is equitable. When someone files for an order of protection or for custody, time matters. Document AI can shorten the time from crisis to remedy, accelerating the journey from "I need help" to "My case is active." Faster initiation means faster relief and better outcomes.

The bottom line: Document AI does not take work away from humans. It takes the friction away from citizens. It turns case initiation from a bureaucratic obstacle course into a guided, supportive, accurate process, especially for people who need help the most. That is Access to Justice.

Robotic Process Automation

Robotic Process Automation, or RPA, is another tool that can dramatically improve Access to Justice, not because it replaces staff, but because it can work around the clock.

RPA bots are essentially digital assistants that perform repetitive, rules-based tasks the same way every single time. And that matters, especially in a justice environment where consistency, speed, and accuracy directly affect people's lives.

RPA helps Access to Justice by reducing delays caused by outdated systems. Many case management systems, especially in government, do not have modern APIs. They were not built for automation. They were not built for scale.

But citizens do not care about system architecture. They just want their filings processed and their cases moving.

RPA bridges that gap.

A bot can log into a legacy system, navigate menus, enter data, attach files, hit submit, and move on to the next case without skipping steps, without fatiguing, without losing focus. That means filings flow faster. Cases open sooner. People get relief sooner.

RPA is not perfect, but it eliminates human error in repetitive tasks. Humans are great at judgment. We are terrible at repetition. RPA thrives on tedium.

When you have repetitive tasks like copying data from one system to another, adding or updating case metadata, routing documents to queues, changing case statuses, attaching supporting documents, or updating indexes, bots do these tasks with perfect consistency.

That means fewer corrections, fewer rejections, and fewer citizens stuck in limbo because a field was missed or mis-typed.

RPA improves transparency and auditability. Every action a bot takes can be logged with timestamps, inputs, outputs, and error conditions.

This creates more clean audit trails than manual work. In a justice system, that level of traceability is essential. It creates trust. It ensures accountability. It removes the perception that things happen 'in the dark.'

RPA supports real-time service across multiple channels.

When you use conversational AI or Document AI, citizens may interact with the system late at night or from remote locations. But someone still has to actually push the filing into the case management system. RPA lets that happen immediately, even outside business hours.

That means a midnight filing does not sit untouched until morning. A remote submission does not wait in a stack.

Emergency cases move the moment they are submitted. For people in crisis, especially domestic violence survivors, that immediate progression matters.

RPA removes the burden of legacy system design from the citizen.

Citizens should not need to know that one system controls filings, another controls images, another controls indexing, and another logs the activity. They just want to submit something and have it work.

"What is taking so long?" "Where is my case in the process?"

RPA stitches those systems together behind the scenes so the front-end experience feels unified and smooth. This is invisible infrastructure, and invisible infrastructure is often the most powerful kind.

RPA does not take jobs from staff. It takes drudgery from staff, delay from citizens, and friction from the justice process. When combined with Document AI and multi-channel access, RPA turns the back-end of case initiation into something fast, consistent, and dependable, which means the front-end experience for citizens becomes more humane, more responsive, and fairer. That is better Access to Justice.

One Bot vs. Object-Oriented Bot Design

The "How" of bot construction is just as critical as the "What."

1. The Trap of the Monolithic Bot

Early automation often relies on "Mega-Bots," single, linear scripts designed to handle a process from end-to-end (e.g., logging in, downloading a filing, reading it via OCR, and updating a database).

- **The Brittle Factor:** In a monolithic design, if the court's login portal changes by one pixel, the entire bot crashes. The OCR capability, though perfectly functional, is trapped inside a dead process.
- **Failure Cascades:** When a monolith fails, it fails "loudly" but unhelpfully. It stops the entire assembly line, requiring a developer to untangle a massive codebase to find the single point of failure.

2. The Case for Object-Oriented (Modular) Design

Object-oriented RPA treats specific capabilities as **independent services** or "workers." Instead of one bot doing everything, you build a fleet of specialized bots that communicate with one another.

The Specialized Fleet

- **The OCR Bot:** Its only job is to turn images into machine-readable text. It does not care where the file came from or where the data is going.
- **The Filing Bot:** Its only job is to navigate the court's E-filing portal.
- **The Validation Bot:** Its only job is to cross-reference data against the Master Knowledge Base.

Why Modular Bots Win

1. **Graceful Failure:** If the court portal changes, only the *Filing Bot* goes offline. Your OCR and Validation bots continue to process the backlog of other tasks.
2. **Reusability:** Once you build a high-performing OCR bot for "Eviction Notices," you can plug that same "object" into your "Foreclosure" process and your "Small Claims" process without rewriting a single line of code.
3. **Independent Scaling:** If you have a surge in filings, you do not need to spin up ten Mega-Bots (which is resource-heavy). You simply spin up ten instances of the specific *OCR Bot* to handle the bottleneck.

3. The Leadership Argument: Risk and Reliability

While implementers focus on the "code," leaders must focus on the **systemic uptime**.

Feature	Monolithic Design (The Risk)	Object-Oriented Design (The Asset)
Maintenance	Requires a "surgeon" to fix the whole system.	Requires a "mechanic" to swap a single part.
Update Speed	High risk; changes can break unrelated steps.	Low risk; updates are isolated to one module.
Total Cost	High long-term cost due to "technical debt."	Higher initial setup, but massive ROI through reuse.
Auditability	Difficult to see where logic failed.	Clear logs for every discrete "object" handoff.

4. Building the "Inter-Bot" Language

The secret to this architecture is the **API-first mindset**. For modular bots to work, they must have standardized ways of passing "batons" (data packets).

The Reliability Thesis: A justice system built on modular RPA is a self-healing system. By decoupling the "intelligence" (OCR/Logic) from the "mechanics" (Navigating Portals), we ensure that a single change in a government website does not paralyze a citizen's access to their legal rights.

This effectively bridges the gap between the "high-trust" governance of your knowledge base and the "boots-on-the-ground" reality of keeping the lights on.

Virtual Agents + RPA

If the **Virtual Agent** is the "face and voice" of digital justice, **RPA** is the "hands and feet." In an Access to Justice context, providing information is only half the battle. A citizen does not just want to know *how* to file a fee waiver; they want the waiver filed.

True end-to-end automation is achieved when the conversational intelligence of a Virtual Agent (VA) is fused with the execution power of RPA.

1. The Integrated Workflow

Neither technology can close the loop in isolation. The VA excels at unstructured conversation but cannot navigate legacy government databases. RPA excels at database navigation but cannot "chat" with a frustrated human to clarify intent.

The Workflow Sequence:

1. **Intake (VA):** The citizen explains their problem in plain language. The VA uses Natural Language Processing (NLP) to

identify the legal "intent" (e.g., "I am being evicted") and gathers the necessary variables (Case number, address, income).

2. **The Digital Handoff:** Once the VA has a complete dataset, it packages this information into a structured payload (JSON/XML) and triggers the RPA bot.
3. **Execution (RPA):** The bot takes the payload, logs into the court portal, fills out the forms, and uploads the documents.
4. **Confirmation (VA):** The RPA bot returns a "Success" or "Failure" signal to the VA, which then notifies the citizen: *"Your filing is complete. Here is your confirmation number."*

2. Architecture of the Handoff

For the handoff to be seamless, the system requires a **Message Queue** or **Orchestrator**. This ensures that if the court portal is down, the VA can tell the citizen, *"I have your info and will submit it as soon as the court system is back online,"* rather than simply crashing.

Object-Oriented Integration

Following the modular design philosophy, the VA should treat the RPA bot as a **Service Object**.

- The VA does not need to know *how* the bot files a document.
- It only needs to know the **Required Input Fields** and the **Expected Output Status**.

3. Human-in-the-Loop (HITL) Checkpoints

In legal processes, "unsupervised" execution is often a bridge too far for risk-averse leaders. Integrating HITL checkpoints into the VA-RPA pipeline provides the necessary "Trust Valve."

Checkpoint Stage	Role of the Human	Why it is Necessary
Pre-Submission	A clerk reviews the data gathered by the VA before the RPA bot hits "Submit."	Ensures the citizen has not misunderstood a legal question.
Exception Handling	A human intervenes if the RPA bot encounters an unrecognized error (e.g., a new pop-up on the court site).	Prevents the system from "spinning" or filing incorrect data.
High-Stakes Verification	Reviewing filings that involve sensitive matters (e.g., domestic violence protective orders).	Adds a layer of legal and ethical oversight to high-risk outcomes.

4. The Stakeholder Impact

- **For Leaders:** This combination represents the transition from a "Help Desk" to a "Digital Courthouse." It reduces the "Two-Tiered" system by providing the same level of administrative support to a Self-Represented Litigant that a high-priced law clerk provides to a firm partner.
- **For Implementers:** The focus shifts from "How do I build a bot?" to "How do I manage the API between the conversation

and the action?" Success is measured by **Completion Rate,** not just "session length."

In an A2J ecosystem, a Virtual Agent without RPA is just a brochure; RPA without a Virtual Agent is just a tool for experts. Together, they create a "Digital Advocate" capable of seeing a citizen through from their first question to their final filing.

MCP

If RPA is the "hands and feet," MCP is the **"standardized nervous system."** It allows your Virtual Agent to securely and consistently plug into the legal knowledge bases, RPA bots, and court databases we have discussed without needing a custom-coded bridge for every single connection.

The Case for MCP in A2J

MCP is an open standard that enables AI models to swap "context" (data and tools) seamlessly. Here is how you can frame it for your two audiences:

1. For Implementers: Solving the "Integration Hell"

Previously, if you wanted your AI to check a specific housing statute and then trigger an RPA bot, you had to write custom "glue code" for both.

- **Plug-and-Play Context:** MCP allows you to build a **Legal Server** once. Any AI model (whether it is the one you use today or a better one released next year) can connect to that server via MCP to pull verified legal "knowledge" or "tools" (like your modular RPA bots).
- **Decoupling the Brain from the Data:** MCP ensures the AI "brain" stays separate from the "legal truth." This prevents the AI from hallucinating laws because it is forced to fetch the law through a strictly defined MCP pipe.

2. For Leaders: Sovereignty and Security

The biggest fear for court leaders is "data leakage" or losing control over their proprietary legal logic to a third-party AI provider.

- **Data Sovereignty:** With MCP, the court keeps its data on its own "MCP server." The AI model only sees what is strictly necessary for the current task. You are not "training" the big AI models on your private data; you are "lending" them context for a split second.
- **Standardized Auditing:** Because MCP is a protocol, every request an AI makes to the legal database is logged in a standardized format. This makes the "Consistency Audit" we discussed earlier much easier to automate.

Why MCP is the "Fairness Protocol"

In the "Fairness" section, we talked about the "Wrong Door" tax. MCP eliminates this at the technical level.

Whether a citizen interacts via a mobile app, a kiosk at the library, or a web portal, all those interfaces connect to the same **MCP Legal Server**. This ensures that the "context" provided to the AI is identical across every channel. It creates a **universal API for Justice**.

The Connective Tissue: MCP as the Universal API for Justice

While Virtual Agents provide the interface and RPA provides the execution, the legal system still faces a fragmented data problem. Every court, law library, and legal aid office has its own "silo" of truth. Traditionally, connecting an AI to these silos required custom-built bridges, an expensive, brittle, and insecure approach.

The **Model Context Protocol (MCP)** replaces these bespoke bridges with a standardized, universal "USB-C port" for legal intelligence.

1. Decoupling the "Brain" from the "Law"

The most dangerous failure in A2J is a "hallucination," where an AI confidently invents a statute. MCP prevents this by structurally separating the AI model (the brain) from the legal data (the source of truth).

- **The MCP Server:** The court or legal aid organization hosts an MCP server containing verified statutes, forms, and procedural rules.
- **The Secure Pipe:** When a citizen asks a question, the AI does not rely on its memory. It reaches through the MCP "pipe" to fetch the specific, verified context from the host's server.
- **The Result:** The AI only "knows" what the server tells it, ensuring that the legal guidance remains grounded in the official record.

2. Eliminating the "Integration Tax" (Implementer Focus)

For implementers, MCP represents the end of "Integration Hell."

- **Standardized Primitives:** MCP uses three core components: **Resources** (the data), **Tools** (the RPA bots), and **Prompts** (the instructions).
- **Interoperability:** If a developer builds an MCP server for "CourtListener" or "PACER" data, any MCP-compatible AI can plug into it in minutes. You no longer need to rewrite your entire back-end just because a better AI model (e.g., moving from GPT-4 to a future model) is released.

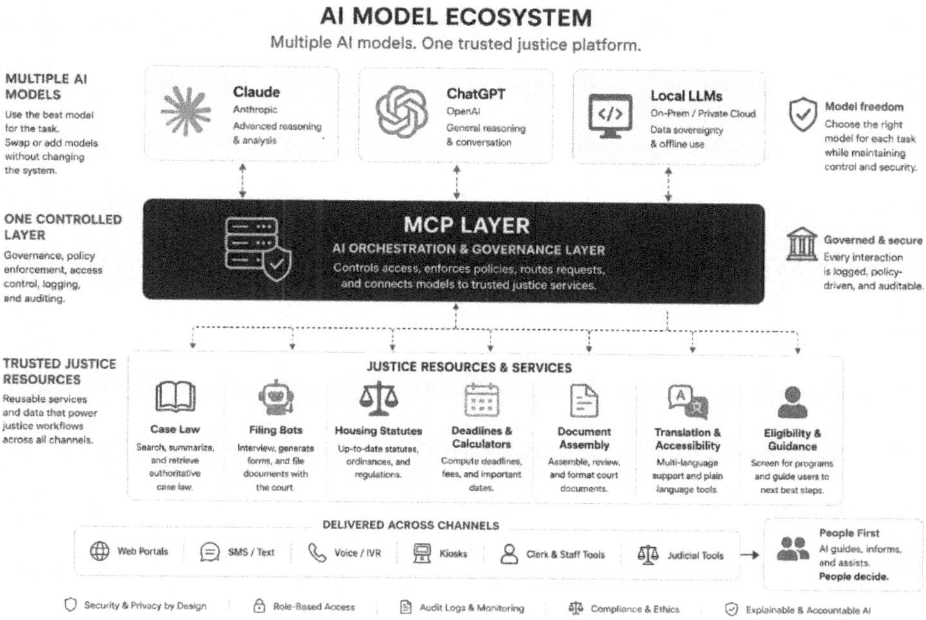

Figure 3: Conceptual AI Governance and Orchestration Layer for Court and Justice Ecosystems.

3. The Sovereignty Argument (Leadership Focus)

For leaders, MCP is about **Control and Security**.

- **Data Sovereignty:** You do not have to upload your proprietary or sensitive data to a tech giant's cloud to "train" a model. You keep your data on your server and only grant the AI "read-only" access to the specific context it needs for a single transaction.

- **The Audit Trail:** MCP provides a standardized log of every time an AI touches a legal resource. This makes the "Justice Audits" we discussed earlier a matter of reviewing standardized logs rather than chasing ghosts in a black box.

4. Toward a "Universal API for Justice"

Imagine a world where every legal jurisdiction provides an **Official MCP Server**.

- A developer building a "Tenant Rights" app does not have to learn the specific API of fifty different states.
- They simply point their app at the standardized MCP endpoints.
- The protocol handles the translation, ensuring that the "Access" in Access to Justice is as simple as plugging in a peripheral.

Justice should not require a custom integration. By adopting MCP, we move from a world of "Digital Islands" to a "Universal Legal Grid," where the most accurate legal information is available to any tool, on any device, at any time.

Our Implementation of Document AI and RPA

At the Clerk of the Superior Court, we created a solution we called Intelligent Capture, an orchestration of technologies that evolved with each phase. In phase one, we replaced the manual work of sorting and barcoding individual case files before scanning. That alone created a 33% reduction in labor.

In phase two, we implemented Nintex for RPA. Our bot would collect case files that were scanned, along with the data payload extracted by AI, open the case management system managed by another agency, and enter the information in a swivel-chair style. This used to require a human to use multiple screens and copy and paste. Our bot could even be throttled to avoid overwhelming the case management system, handle its own password resets, and not depend on the position of fields on the screen. AI identified case and document types after scanning, extracting features like party information, dates, and case numbers. When we combined that feature extraction with robotic process automation, we achieved a 73% reduction in labor overall. This worked beautifully for the volumes of recordation coming across the counters.

Forms Automation

Our next improvement opportunity involved integrating with the Superior Court's Law Library Resource Center.

The law library is a delicate balance: offering assistance without ever creating the perception of advice.

The court cannot ever be seen as suggesting that a citizen should file a form. But if a citizen wants to file a form, how do we best assist them?

How do we intercept the printing of that form only to have it scanned right back in?

This is where forms automation, AI assistants, and Document AI can work together. Forms are persistent barriers in the justice system. They seem simple, but for many citizens, they are confusing, intimidating, and easy to get wrong. Courts walk a very fine line: they can assist, but they cannot advise. They can help someone understand a process, but they cannot tell them what to file. Forms automation, when carefully designed, can honor that boundary while still dramatically improving Access to Justice.

Forms automation reduces cognitive load. Most legal forms are written for lawyers, not the public, and are packed with jargon, cross-references, and questions that assume the reader already understands legal structure. There is a reason humans bring paper filings to the counter rather than submitting digitally. When they slide that paper across the counter, and the clerk does not look at them like they have done something wrong, they know they are at least close. Those quality control moments must always exist in automation. Forms automation addresses this by breaking forms into one question at a time, in plain-language prompts with dynamic guidance and contextual hints. Citizens do not have to sift through a ten-page packet of instructions; they just answer questions, and the system quietly handles the complexity underneath. This reduces anxiety, reduces mistakes, and reduces the sense of "I am doing something wrong."

Incomplete or incorrectly filled forms are among the biggest reasons filings are rejected. Forms automation can validate required fields, ensure names and dates match across pages, attach the right supporting documents, prevent contradictory answers, and warn users if something important is missing. Instead of a clerk having to send someone away to start over and lose days or weeks, the system catches issues before the citizen ever submits. It also improves accessibility for people with diverse needs: screen readers for the visually impaired, voice input for low-literacy users, multilingual support, larger text, simplified layouts, and step-by-step pacing for people with ADHD, dyslexia, or anxiety. For neurodivergent citizens or those with disabilities, the traditional PDF form is a wall. Automated forms transform that wall into a guided pathway while preserving the legal boundary between assistance and advice—that tightrope walk.

Most importantly, forms automation eliminates the print–scan–print–scan loop. One of the biggest inefficiencies in traditional courts is the cycle of a citizen downloading a PDF, printing it, handwriting answers, bringing it in, having a clerk scan it, and then having AI or staff retype the same information. Forms automation breaks that loop entirely. When combined with Document AI and RPA, it becomes part of an end-to-end experience where the citizen gets help understanding a form, the form is completed correctly, the filing is initiated automatically, and the case is created in the CMS.

Forms automation is not about making courts more efficient for the sake of efficiency. It is about removing one of the biggest sources of frustration in the entire justice pipeline: fear, delay, and inequity.

When you automate forms the right way, with clarity, neutrality, accessibility, and plain language, you help people begin a journey they might never have started at all.

That is real Access to Justice.

Chapter 9 Designing for Humans

AI to Understand Gaps in Access to Justice

AI can act as an early-warning system for access gaps, more than reactive, it can be diagnostic. When patterns emerge, spikes in confusion about a form, recurring questions about a process, or citizens repeatedly stuck at the same step, those signals can surface pain points to court leadership. Instead of waiting for complaints or backlogs, administrators can see the invisible friction that keeps people from progressing. AI reveals where systems confuse, exclude, or overwhelm, and in doing so becomes a healer of systems.

Legal Research AI: The Professional Tool and the Public Risk

There is no category of AI adoption moving faster in the legal sector right now than legal research. Westlaw CoCounsel, Harvey, Lexis+ AI, and a growing list of competitors are changing how attorneys prepare cases, how law clerks draft bench memos, and how legal aid organizations serve clients they could never have reached before. For courts thinking about workforce and efficiency, this is the most immediate and visible shift. A law clerk who used to spend two days pulling cases for a motion hearing can do it in twenty minutes. That does not eliminate the clerk. It changes what the clerk does with the other day, plus seven hours and forty minutes. Courts that understand this early will redirect that capacity toward the work that has always been underfunded: the human judgment, the nuanced explanation, the citizen who needs someone to slow down and listen. Courts that do not will cut the position and discover too late that the judgment they automated away was the part that mattered.

The harder design question is what happens when these tools face a citizen rather than an attorney. Legal research AI is built on an assumption: that the person using it can evaluate what it returns. An attorney reading a CoCounsel summary knows to check whether the cited case is still good law, whether the jurisdiction is right, and whether the holding actually applies to their facts. That evaluation is not instinctive. It is trained. A Self-Represented Litigant reading the same summary may not know that a case was overruled last year, or that a persuasive opinion from another circuit carries no weight in their court, or that the AI has subtly mischaracterized the holding because the question was ambiguous. They will often take the output as authoritative because it sounds authoritative. The fluency of the tool creates a false confidence in users who lack the background to question it.

This does not mean courts should keep legal research AI away from Self-Represented Litigants. It means they need to be honest about the scaffolding required before deployment is safe. A citizen-facing legal research tool needs constrained output—plain-language summaries rather than raw citations, clear statements of what the tool cannot do, and explicit prompts to seek human review before acting on what they read. It needs a Human-in-the-Loop checkpoint before any output is used to make a filing decision. And it needs to be transparent with the user: this is a starting point, not a finish line. Courts that deploy legal research AI for citizens without that scaffolding are not expanding Access to Justice. They are replacing one barrier with a more sophisticated one.

For legal aid organizations, the calculus is different. A trained paralegal or supervising attorney using Harvey or CoCounsel to serve ten times the clients in the same time is one of the most genuinely transformative applications of AI in the Access to Justice space. The tool is still in the hands of someone who can evaluate it. The leverage is enormous. If there is one category where courts and legal aid organizations should be moving urgently, it is here—not by giving citizens the raw tool, but by using it to dramatically expand the capacity of the professionals who serve them.

Human-Centered Design

There is a misconception that technology makes the justice system less human. The truth is the opposite: when used responsibly, AI gives humanity back to the system.

When routine work is automated, clerks can manage exceptions. When chatbots absorb repetitive questions, staff can focus on the human aspects that calm anxious litigants. When filings move automatically, judges can focus on reasoning instead of paperwork. Technology cannot replace empathy, but it can create the conditions for it. That is the quiet realization we rarely take note of: justice is more than a matter of law; it is a matter of tone, of compassion, of patience. AI, when properly implemented, gives those qualities room to breathe.

Here in the U.S., frameworks like the NIST AI Risk Management Framework and the White House AI Bill of Rights provide guidance for safe, ethical implementation. Do not think of them as red tape—they are more like lifelines for how to build trust. Because in justice, perception is as powerful as performance. People must believe the system is fair before they can believe it is effective.

As we began developing advanced solutions, we came up with a series of principles that helped guide our design decisions. These were not arbitrarily chosen. These emerged from deep design sessions where we considered the impact of journey progression on citizen outcomes.

1. A Solution Must Survive Its Creator

Anything we build must be built on a technology that any other technologist with a reasonable skill set could continue to support. In kind, when moving from development to operations, the solution must be manageable by an operations team without heavy reliance on the creator(s). There will, of course, be a period of transition we call "early life support" where the developer(s) help to triage issues while the support team gains the required aptitude, but that is not indefinite.

2. The "Never Repeat" Rule

Sometimes stated as, a user should not have to tell their story twice, or a user should never have to start their journey over. There is nothing more demoralizing than explaining a painful personal history to an intake system, whether AI or human, only to be told by the next person in line: "Start from the beginning." Data persistence is not just a technical feature; it is a form of respect for the user's time and trauma.

3. The Principle of Trauma-Informed Inquiry

For many, legal issues are inextricably linked to the worst moments of their lives, such as eviction, domestic violence, or the threat of losing their children. A trauma-informed interface avoids "cold" or "interrogative" questioning that can trigger a fight-or-flight response. Instead, it uses neutral, supportive framing and offers transparency about why a question is being asked. By allowing users to control the pace and providing "off-ramps" to human support, we ensure the technology acts as a stabilizer, not a stressor.

4. A Solution Should Relieve Cognitive Load, Not Create One

A solution intended for untrained user experiences should not require the user to learn new skills to use. Drafting technologies require users to understand drafting prior to use. A customer should only need to know how to be a customer with no prior training.

Mapping applications show this well. A user should not have to understand "layers" or spatial relationships to know that a point inside a polygon means the district they are in. That is a cognitive exercise better suited for natural language experiences.

5. The Danger of "Screen-First" Thinking

Poorly designed interfaces often increase cognitive load rather than reducing it. If a system forces a user through a complex login screen before they have even received any help, they will leave. Furthermore, heavy reliance on visual-only menus can alienate those with different accessibility needs and may even violate the spirit of Title III of the ADA. We must design for the ear and the heart, not just the eye.

6. The Customer Determines Value

We often speculate how transformative a solution will be. In reality, only the end user, the customer, the citizen, the constituent, knows how valuable our solution is to their experience.

7. Value-First Privacy

Trust is a currency that must be earned. Prioritizing a user's data privacy before requesting sensitive information builds the foundation for an honest exchange. When we ask about case numbers or dates too early, the system feels like a bureaucratic hurdle. When we offer help first, the system feels like a partner.

8. The Cost of Coercion

Forcing users to accept system decisions erodes trust. True agency means granting users the power to say "no" or "not yet." If a digital system is so rigid that users feel they must bypass it to find a "real" human, they will forever favor the more expensive, traditional lines of business. A digital tool should be an express lane, not a trap.

9. Avoiding the "Algorithmic Filter"

Unchecked automation is dangerous. It can reinforce existing biases and cause premature case closures, leaving marginalized communities without the human review they deserve. We cannot allow technology to become a high-tech version of the "filtering" systems that have kept people out of courthouses for decades.

10. The Human Safety Net

The absence of clear communication and human involvement makes any digital journey inaccessible. We have all experienced the frustration of a chatbot that does not understand us, leading to the desperate plea: "I would like to speak to a human agent, please." If the digital path is confusing and there is no human backup, the user is not just lost; they are stranded.

These principles don't mean much until they are tested against real people, in real conditions, with real stakes. Principle 6 says the customer determines value. The only way to honor that is to put the system in front of customers before you ship it. When we built Cleo's voice channel, we did exactly that.

When creating a voice channel for Cleo, we looked at the primary demographics of Maricopa County. Based on our population, we recruited individuals to test our solution, matching their gender, age, ethnicity, and spoken language. This was to better understand how effective our voice channel would be across diverse life experiences, regional dialects, and generational engagement expectations.

Utterances varied greatly for similar tasks. Trampling (when the user interrupts the AI) and pauses in speech (the silence between spoken sentences or at the end of a sentence) were interpreted differently. Some users were able to see past clunky mechanics to see future value after more refinement, while others were completely turned off by their experience with the AI.

Chapter 10 Vendor Selection and Procurement

The Build vs. Buy vs. Bargain Framework

Before you sign anything, you need to know which of three roads you are on, because each one leads somewhere very different. The choice comes down to **control, cost, and risk**. A "bargain" solution or a "home-grown" build might look attractive on a first-year budget sheet, but the long-term architectural debt and legal exposure can be significant.

1. Strategic Comparison Matrix

Feature	**Build Your Own**	**Bargain Bots**	**Enterprise AI**
Initial Cost	Lowest (Direct)	Low (Plug-and-Play)	Highest (Acquisition)
Maintenance	High (Entirely on you)	Low (Limited scope)	Lowest (Vendor managed)
Data Ingestion	Full control	Website only	Omnivorous (PDFs, Video, SharePoint)

Feature	Build Your Own	Bargain Bots	Enterprise AI
Channels	Multi (if you build them)	Website Widget Only	Omni-Channel (SMS, Voice, Social)
Customization	Infinite but difficult	Very Limited	High (Built-in tools)
Analytics	Must build manually	Basic/Non-existent	Advanced Dashboards
Legal Indemnity	**None**	Rare/Limited	**Included**

2. Identifying the Three Paths

A. Build Your Own: You Own It All

This path gives you total sovereignty but demands total responsibility. Your team is not just building a legal tool; they are building a software company.

- **The Trap:** It is cheaper to start, but exponentially more expensive to extend. You are responsible for every API integration, the front-end UI, and the voice/SMS gateways.

- **The Risk:** You carry 100% of the legal risk. If the system gives damaging advice, there is no vendor to share the liability.

B. Bargain Bots: The "Widget" Trap

Often offered as part of web hosting or as simple plugins, these are enticing for their "plug-and-play" nature.

- **The Scope:** They are typically "one-trick ponies," functional for a website chat bubble but incapable of reaching citizens via SMS or social media.
- **The Constraint:** They usually only "read" your public website. They cannot ingest your internal helpdesk data or private legal repositories, making them shallow "brochure-bots" rather than true A2J tools.

C. Enterprise AI: Someone Else Keeps the Lights On

Enterprise solutions are built for scale and security. While the sticker price is higher, the "Cost per Resolution" is often lower because the infrastructure is pre-built and managed.

- **The Advantage:** These systems provide **Omni-channel** support (meaning the conversation stays the same whether the user is on a phone or a laptop) and advanced analytics to prove the system is working.
- **The Safety Net:** They provide legal indemnity and robust vendor support, shifting the technical and legal burden away from your internal team.

3. The "Hidden" Decision Drivers

When evaluating these three options, two factors should outweigh the initial price tag:

1. **Legal Indemnity:** In an Access to Justice context, providing "wrong" information can have life-altering consequences for a

citizen. Enterprise vendors stand behind their models; in a "Build" or "Bargain" scenario, your organization stands alone.

2. **The Contextual Reach:** A bargain bot that exists only on your website ignores the significant share of the population that relies on **SMS and mobile-first** communication. Enterprise systems are designed to go where the users are, not just where your web server is.

Do not buy for the launch; buy for the life cycle. A "bargain" today is often a "rebuild" tomorrow.

The matrix above tells you what each path costs to start. Here is what each one looks like by year two, which is the year most courts don't budget for.

Build Your Own in year two means you are maintaining everything you built in year one while simultaneously trying to keep pace with a technology landscape that moved significantly while you were building. The developer or team who built the system becomes the system's permanent dependency. When they leave, institutional knowledge leaves with them. You will also discover in year two that every new channel, every new language, and every new integration is a new project. The initial build was not a product. It was a foundation that requires ongoing construction. If your team has the capacity and the mandate for that, build. If they do not, this path will quietly consume them.

Bargain Bots in year two often reveal their ceiling at the moment you most need them to scale. A service expansion, a high-profile case that drives traffic, a new language requirement from leadership, and the widget cannot follow. You are also likely to discover that the vendor who was enthusiastic during the sales process is difficult to reach for support after the contract is signed. The low initial cost creates a false baseline. When the rebuild conversation arrives, and it will, the cost is not just the new system. It is the time your team spent managing the old one, the data you cannot export cleanly, and the trust you lost with users who experienced its limitations.

Enterprise AI in year two should look like a system that is improving rather than one you are fighting to maintain. The vendor is managing the infrastructure, releasing updates, and handling the integrations that would have consumed your team's capacity in either of the other paths. The risk in year two is complacency. Enterprise contracts can create a dependency that feels comfortable until renewal arrives and the pricing has changed. Fight for multi-year rate locks in the original contract. Build in performance benchmarks with exit ramps if those benchmarks are not met. The vendor relationship should feel like a partnership with accountability, not a subscription you cannot cancel.

Oranges to Orangutans

Before you can evaluate a vendor's proposal or compare two competing technologies, you have to understand exactly what you are being charged for. In traditional software procurement, we are used to buying "seats" or "licenses," but the generative AI marketplace has moved the goalposts. You are not just buying access; you are buying the raw material of thought. If you do not understand the underlying unit of measurement, you cannot predict your first-year budget, and you certainly cannot compare two quotes that might look identical on the surface but are actually as different as oranges and orangutans.

In the world of AI and legal tech, **tokens** are the fundamental currency of intelligence. For leaders, they represent the "cost of justice" and the unit of billing; for implementers, they represent the "memory limit" and the technical constraints of the system. Every interaction, from a user asking about a court date to the AI reviewing a fifty-page lease, is converted into these digital units before a single calculation is made.

1. What is a Token?

A token is not necessarily a "word." It is a sequence of characters an AI model uses to process information.

- **The Breakdown:** Common words like "law" might be one token, but complex legal terms like "usufructuary" or "quasi-contractual" might be broken into three or four tokens.
- **The Rule of Thumb:** In English, 1,000 tokens is approximately **750 words,** roughly the length of a two-page legal brief.

2. The Context Window (The "Mental Workspace")

For the implementer audience, the most critical concept is the **Context Window**. This is the maximum number of tokens the AI can "hold in its head" at one time.

- **The Intake Problem:** If a user uploads fifty pages of medical records and twenty pages of lease agreements, the total token count might exceed the AI's window. When this happens, the AI "forgets" the beginning of the conversation to make room for the end.
- **The Precision Risk:** In a legal context, if the AI "forgets" a specific clause from page one because the context window is full, it may provide dangerously incorrect advice. This is why **RAG (Retrieval-Augmented Generation)** is used to feed only the most relevant tokens into the window at any given time.

3. The Economics of Tokens (Leadership Perspective)

Leaders must view tokens as a **utility cost**, similar to electricity or postage.

Token Type	Responsibility	Economic Impact
Input Tokens	The prompt and the "context" (statutes/facts) provided to the AI.	Higher costs for "heavy" legal research involving long documents.
Output Tokens	The response generated by the AI.	Controlled by setting limits on how long the AI's "advice" can be.
Caching	Reusing frequently accessed legal data (e.g., the State Constitution).	Reduces costs by not "paying" for the same tokens twice.

4. Why Tokens Matter for Fairness

Tokens create a hidden **"Complexity Tax"** on justice:

1. **Language Bias:** Non-English languages (like Spanish or Mandarin) often require more tokens to express the same legal concept as English. This can make AI services subtly more expensive or less performant for non-English speakers.
2. **The Verbosity Trap:** If an AI is poorly "prompted," it may waste tokens on polite filler rather than legal substance, draining the budget of a legal aid organization.
3. **The "Long-Tail" Case:** Complex cases with thousands of pages of evidence require more "token overhead," potentially

making AI assistance harder to scale for the very people who need it most.

To the AI, a legal right is just a string of tokens. To the citizen, those tokens are the difference between being heard and being ignored. Managing tokens efficiently is the technical prerequisite for managing justice equitably.

Model Context Protocol (MCP), which we discussed earlier, is a primary way to manage "token bloat" by only fetching the exact legal tokens needed for a specific query, rather than dumping an entire law library into the AI's context window.

The Procurement Paradox: Budgeting for the Unpredictable

Budgeting for your first year of AI implementation is like trying to buy gas for a car when you do not know the mileage, the destination, or the price per gallon. Most vendors use one of three primary pricing pillars. Comparing them is often an "apples-to-oranges-to-bricks" exercise.

1. The Three Pricing Pillars

Vendors typically obscure their true costs within one of these models:

Seat-Based (Traditional)	Consumption-Based (The Meter)	Infrastructure-Based (The Engine)
Metrics: Number of users per month; Number of source websites/files.	**Metrics:** Input tokens (words in); Output tokens (words out); Source material tokens.	**Metrics:** Data storage required; Computation power (GPU/CPU); Dedicated performance tiers.
Risk: Paying for "ghost users" who do not utilize the	**Risk:** Total budget volatility. A single "viral" legal crisis can	**Risk:** Over-provisioning. Paying for high performance during low-

Seat-Based (Traditional)	Consumption-Based (The Meter)	Infrastructure-Based (The Engine)
tool; arbitrary caps on data.	blow your annual budget in a week.	traffic periods (nights/weekends).

2. The Fallacy of the "Short Input"

Shorter user queries are not automatically cheaper. In a token-based world, the math is more complicated than it looks.

- **The Ambiguity Tax:** If a user provides a two-word input like *"Eviction help,"* the AI must ask five follow-up questions to resolve the ambiguity (Where? Why? When? Who?). Each of those exchanges incurs more input and output tokens.
- **The "Life Story" Value:** While a user who provides a 2,000-word account of their legal situation uses more tokens upfront, they often provide enough context for the AI to solve the problem in **one single, high-quality turn**.
- **The Lesson:** Do not optimize for brevity; optimize for **resolution efficiency**.

3. The "Back Lot Tour" Test

During a demo, do not just watch the scripted "Happy Path." You need to see the engine room.

- **The Pivot Test:** Ask the vendor to use a sanitized copy of *your* data—right now.
    - If they can upload it and show results instantly, the system is **flexible and robust**.
    - If they say, *"We need to take this back to our engineers,"* the system is **brittle and bespoke**. You are not buying a product; you are buying a long-term professional services contract.

- **The "Confidence" Question:** Ask what happens when the AI is unsure. Does it hallucinate a "best guess," or does it have a hard "low-confidence" trigger that routes the user to a human?

- **The Data Noise Test:** Ask how the system handles **contradictory data**. If you have two versions of a housing statute in your knowledge base, how does the AI decide which one is the "Source of Truth"?

4. Continuity and Sovereignty

In the volatile world of AI startups, "High-Trust" means planning for the vendor's disappearance.

- **The "Going Under" Protocol:** If the vendor goes out of business, who owns the logic? Can you export your fine-tuned prompts, your embeddings, and your knowledge base structure?

- **Data Portability:** Ensure your contract includes a "Right to Retrieval" clause. You must be able to get your data back in a machine-readable format (not just a dump of PDFs) if you decide to switch vendors.

5. Watch Out For... (The Red Flags)

- **The "Unlimited" Trap:** If a vendor offers "unlimited tokens," read the fine print. There is always a "Fair Use Policy" that acts as a hidden ceiling.

- **Proprietary Lock-in:** Avoid vendors that do not support open standards such as **MCP**. If they force you into a proprietary ecosystem, you are stuck with their price hikes forever.

- **Black Box Support:** If they cannot explain *why* an AI gave a specific wrong answer during a pilot, they will not be able to fix it when it happens in production.

- **Hidden RAG Costs:** Some vendors charge for the "indexing" of your data (turning your websites into tokens) every time you update it. If you have a frequently changing legal knowledge base, this "update tax" can be ruinous.

If a vendor cannot give you a clear, transparent answer on their cost model, they are not just a financial risk—they are an **operational risk**. In Access to Justice, an unpredictable cost model eventually leads to a "shuttering" of services for the people who need them most.

There is one more factor most procurement conversations never reach: public trust. Citizens notice headlines. They will gauge their trust in your technology choice as much as you do, and sometimes more. If you select a platform built by a company with a poor reputation for privacy or data ethics, that reputation follows you into every interaction. Citizens may fear their questions are being collected, profiled, or sold, even when they are not. That fear does not require proof. It only requires suspicion, and suspicion kills engagement. In Access to Justice, low engagement means people who needed help did not ask for it.

This is one reason we selected IBM Watson for our conversational AI. We did not just evaluate IBM on technical merit. We evaluated what IBM meant to the people we were trying to serve. In 1996, IBM's Deep Blue lost to Garry Kasparov in a six-game match. They came back the following year, rebuilt the system, and won. In February 2011, IBM's Watson supercomputer defeated Jeopardy's two greatest champions, Ken Jennings and Brad Rutter, in a special televised tournament. IBM SlamTracker has been the scoring platform for Wimbledon for years. IBM's Watsonx powers the official Scuderia Ferrari app, turning complex race telemetry into insights for fans. For more than thirty years, IBM has been the technology partner of the Masters Tournament. Those moments span generations, and citizens carry them. When a seventy-year-old walks up to a court kiosk and sees IBM, something in them relaxes. They have heard that name their whole lives in contexts that worked. It was my opportunity to build on that. Their trust became our trust.

Designing a Pilot That Tells You Something True

A pilot is only useful if it tests the right things. Most vendor pilots test the happy path on clean data in ideal conditions. That is not what your production environment looks like. A pilot that tells you something true puts the system under realistic stress from the first week.

Set a fixed window. Ninety days is the right length for a court AI pilot. Long enough to see the system under varied conditions, including edge cases and high-volume periods. Short enough that you have not committed resources you cannot recover if the result is negative. Anything shorter than sixty days is a demo. Anything longer than six months without a formal evaluation checkpoint is a relationship, not a pilot.

Define success before you start. This sounds obvious and is almost universally skipped. Before the pilot begins, write down the specific numbers that would constitute success and the specific numbers that would constitute failure. Task completion rate. Escalation rate to human staff. User satisfaction if you can measure it. Knowledge base accuracy against a defined test set. If you do not define these before the pilot, you will spend the evaluation period arguing about which metrics matter and the vendor will always have a number that looks good.

Use your real data from day one. Sanitized versions of your actual knowledge base, your real form types, your real question patterns from citizen interactions. Not sample data the vendor provides. Your data will expose gaps, conflicts, and edge cases that the vendor's sample data was specifically designed to avoid exposing.

Test the failure modes explicitly. Ask questions the system should not answer. Submit documents with contradictory information. Try to get the system to cross topic boundaries. Ask a housing question in the middle of a family court conversation. These are the moments that reveal whether the system was built carefully or built for demos. In a justice context, how a system fails is as important as how it succeeds.

Know when to stop. If the system fails the predefined success metrics at the thirty-day checkpoint, stop the pilot. Not pause it. Stop it. A vendor who argues that thirty days is not enough time to see the system properly has sold you a system that requires thirty days to hide its problems. A well-built system performs at or near its ceiling on day one. Tuning improves it at the margins. It does not transform it.

Before You Sign: Questions That Belong in Every Contract Conversation

The Back Lot Tour Test and the Red Flags section give you what to watch for during demos. These are the questions to ask before the contract is signed, when you still have leverage. Once the ink is dry, the answers to these questions become the terms you live with.

On cost: What is the per-unit cost at twice our projected volume? What triggers an overage and how are we notified before we hit it? Is there a rate lock available and for how long? What happens to our pricing at renewal if we have become dependent on the system?

On data: Who owns the citizen interaction data? Is it used to train the vendor's models? Can we get a contractual prohibition on that? If we leave, what does data retrieval look like and how long does it take? Is our knowledge base exportable in a machine-readable format or only as a PDF dump?

On performance: What SLA governs uptime and what is the remedy if it is missed? How are model updates communicated and how much notice do we receive before a change that might affect our knowledge base? Who do we call at 2 AM on the night before a high-profile hearing if the system goes down?

On exit: What does the termination clause look like? How long is the off-boarding period? If the vendor is acquired or goes out of business, what are our contractual protections? Is there a technology escrow for the system logic and prompt architecture?

On accountability: Who is liable if the system provides incorrect legal information that harms a citizen? Is that liability covered by the indemnification clause and what are its limits? Can we see the indemnification terms before we sign the master agreement?

A vendor who answers these questions clearly and completely is a vendor you can work with. A vendor who deflects, qualifies everything, or tells you the legal team handles that is showing you exactly what the relationship will feel like after you have signed.

Value-Added Resellers (VAR) vs. Request for Proposal (RFP)

For government entities, we are bound by procurement rules. We have limits on the amount of money we can spend and where we can purchase from.

Implementers, if you know what you need, look to your value-added resellers (VARs) that already have contract vehicles, lean on them. If what you want to do is unfamiliar to you or you do not have any VAR options, you will need to go through the request for proposal (RFP) process, which is difficult and sometimes results in someone else choosing the technology you will have to implement.

There is a formal mechanism for purchasing the thing you know you need when no one else provides it, called a sole-source or brand-name justification. The names vary by jurisdiction, but the principle is the same: you are arguing that competition is impractical because the solution is unique. You will need to be able to prove you know what you need, why you need it, and why your chosen solution is the only suitable one.

Always check with your procurement office before engaging a vendor. In most cases, you can ask a vendor for a rough cost estimate without triggering procurement obligations. You never know, it may be cheap and easy to expense. However, if it is a costly product and you have to go through an RFP, you could be harming yourself by engaging too early.

Chapter 11 Future of AI in Justice

So, what should the future of AI in justice look like?

Not courts with fewer people in them. Not clerks replaced by screens. Not judges whose decisions are made by an algorithm. The future I am describing is one where a single mother in a rural county can whisper a question into her phone at midnight and get a real answer. Where a man who does not speak English can file a protective order without needing an interpreter to be scheduled. Where the person who never made it to the courthouse door finally gets to walk through it. That is the vision. Everything in this chapter is in service of it.

The court workforce is not going away. It is changing. The fear that AI will eliminate jobs is understandable and widely held. Bentley University and Gallup found that roughly three-quarters of Americans expect AI to reduce the number of jobs over the next decade.[3] The data so far tells a more complicated story. Researchers from Scale AI and the Center for AI Safety found that the best-performing AI system completed only 2.5% of real-world work projects tested.[4] The Remote Labor Index concluded that current models are not close to automating real jobs in the economy.[5] AI is not replacing your clerk or your judge. Not now. But it is changing what excellence looks like in every role it touches.

Think about what the best clerk already does. They do not just process filings—they read the room. They notice the person at the counter who is shaking. They answer the question behind the question. That judgment, that empathy, that ability to see a human being instead of a case number—AI cannot replicate it, and it should not try. What AI

---

[3] Bentley University & Gallup. (2024). *Confident but unprepared: Workers' readiness for an AI-driven economy.* https://www.bentley.edu/gallup

[4] Mazeika, M., et al. (2025). *Remote Labor Index: Measuring AI automation of remote work.* Scale AI & Center for AI Safety. https://www.remotelabor.ai

[5] Mazeika, M., et al. (2025). *Remote Labor Index: Measuring AI automation of remote work.* Scale AI & Center for AI Safety. https://www.remotelabor.ai

can do is clear the repetitive, mechanical work that buries the clerk under volume, so that judgment has room to operate. The future court professional is not someone whose job was automated away. It is someone whose job got more human because the machine took the tedium.

For those in leadership and implementation roles, the shift is different but equally real. Legacy software was predictable: you pushed a button, you got a predictable response. AI agents work more like staff: skilled, adaptable, occasionally imperfect, and in need of direction, context, and oversight to stay on track. The new competency is not using AI. It is supervising it, knowing when to trust the output and when to question it, when to delegate a full workflow and when to decompose it into smaller supervised steps, when the system is performing and when it is silently degrading. Courts that cultivate that judgment now will be positioned well. Courts that wait and assume the technology will manage itself will find out the hard way that it does not.

AI should act as a navigator, not an authority. That principle does not change as the technology matures. A well-designed system walks alongside the user, breaking complicated processes into understandable steps, pointing out which forms exist and explaining what each process involves, without ever crossing the line into legal advice. It does not try to imitate an attorney, invent rules, or speak outside its scope. It knows its boundaries and stays within them. Its purpose is not to override human expertise but to help people make sense of information that feels inaccessible or overwhelming. When done right, AI becomes the bridge between confusion and clarity, not the wall between citizen and court. This is the distinction between guidance and advice, and it must always remain intact.

The next wave of tools will give us personalization without prying. A citizen will not have to create an account or share personal data to get help with a simple question. An intelligent assistant will tailor its responses to intent, not identity, understanding what you need in this moment without storing who you are after you leave. It will remember what you are doing, but not who you are, once you are done. That is not a technical limitation. It is a design choice. Support without surveillance. Assistance without over-collection. For communities that have long distrusted "the system," that distinction is not subtle. It is the difference between a tool that helps and a tool that watches.

The next evolution will not look like a chatbot at all. It will be ambient—quietly surrounding the citizen, available the moment help is needed, but never intrusive. Ambient AI does not demand tech literacy. Imagine walking into a public library and seeing a simple kiosk that says, "Need legal help? Start here." Or asking your smart speaker at home, "What do I do if my landlord will not return my deposit?" and being safely guided to official resources and forms. Imagine a multilingual kiosk in a rural courthouse lobby that reads a form aloud, line by line, while automatically filling in the digital copy. It does not require a login. It simply exists wherever the need appears. This is justice that comes to you—you do not have to go find it.

The key to ambient design is consistency and transparency. The system only activates when invited. It does not listen all the time—it listens when asked. It simply assists without tracking or judgment. For communities still fearful of "the system," that subtle distinction is everything. It transforms AI from a symbol of control into a tool of empowerment.

As AI evolves, we move from stand-alone bots to coordinated networks of specialized agents. Residents will not think in terms of "departments." They will simply ask questions. One agent might handle animal services, another might cover court hours, and another might help with property records. Behind the scenes, these agents collaborate while staying in their own lanes, creating a seamless experience for the resident without any risk of mixing sensitive information across domains. Restraint is critical here. A model may be capable of answering a legal question, but that does not mean it should—the cost of a single incorrect answer can be irreversible. This is why routing justice questions to a deterministic, rule-based system remains the safest choice. That orchestration is the key to digital trust. It says: "We will help you, but we will also protect you."

For Maria, none of that architecture is visible. She doesn't know which agent answered her question about the broken water heater and which one confirmed the fee waiver. She doesn't know what a deterministic system is or why her housing question was handled differently than her question about court hours. She just knows that when she needed help, something helped her. That is the right outcome. The complexity belongs to us. The simplicity belongs to her.

The future of AI in justice will be written through collaboration: between technologists, judges, clerks, researchers, advocates, and the communities they serve. No single vendor, agency, or model owns this mission. Justice is a shared public good, and AI must remain its servant, not its sovereign.

Think of AI as infrastructure, like roads or power lines. Its value comes from what it connects, not what it replaces. If we treat AI systems as civic infrastructure, we will plan for maintenance, oversight, transparency, and public input. We build longevity without chasing novelty. We do not install tools in secret; we design them in daylight. Imagine every county, every court, every agency sharing interoperable components: a single knowledge base, a single trust layer, a single ethics framework. That is how we build an AI system that scales justice, not just software.

Access to justice has never truly been about technology. It is about people—about fairness, dignity, and trust. Technology is simply the bridge that helps us reach one another. When I think back to the Appalachian communities where I grew up, people an hour away from the nearest courthouse, people who viewed "the law" as something to fear, not to seek, I imagine what it would mean for them to whisper a question into their phone and hear a calm, helpful response. No courtroom. No intimidation. No judgment. Just help. That is what we are building toward. A world where distance, language, anxiety, and literacy no longer determine who gets justice. A world where the courthouse is not a building, but a network of compassion, available everywhere, at any time.

The next generation of AI, ambient, responsible, and inclusive, can make that world real. It will not make justice faster just for the sake of speed. It will make it better, fairer, and more human.

The promise of AI in justice is not efficiency.

It is equity.

It is clarity.

It is dignity.

If we design these systems intentionally, with humility, with oversight, and with the understanding that every citizen interaction carries weight, we can build a future where Access to Justice is not a privilege or a gamble. It becomes the default, not the exception.

That is not a distant dream. That is what is next.

Bibliography

National Center for Education Statistics. (2023). *Program for the International Assessment of Adult Competencies (PIAAC): State and county estimates.* U.S. Department of Education. https://nces.ed.gov/surveys/piaac/state-county-estimates.asp

Eysenck, M. W., Derakshan, N., Santos, R., & Calvo, M. G. (2007). Anxiety and cognitive performance: Attentional control theory. *Emotion, 7*(2), 336–353. https://doi.org/10.1037/1528-3542.7.2.336

Bentley University & Gallup. (2024). *Confident but unprepared: Workers' readiness for an AI-driven economy.* https://www.bentley.edu/gallup

Mazeika, M., et al. (2025). *Remote Labor Index: Measuring AI automation of remote work.* Scale AI & Center for AI Safety. https://www.remotelabor.ai

About the Author

Aaron Judy grew up in Appalachia, an hour from the nearest courthouse, in communities where the law felt like something that belonged to other people. That experience never left him.

As Chief of Innovation and AI at the Maricopa County Clerk of the Superior Court, one of the largest court systems in the United States, Aaron led the deployment of Cleo, an IBM Watson-powered virtual assistant that helped Self-Represented Litigants navigate the court system across multiple channels and languages. His team developed Intelligent Capture, an AI and robotic process automation solution that reduced document processing labor by 73%. He represented the clerk's office on the State Subcommittee for AI, where he worked alongside judges, administrators, and policymakers to shape how Arizona approaches artificial intelligence in government.

He now serves as Chief of Innovation and Emerging Technologies for Maricopa County's Enterprise Technology and Innovation department, where his work expanded beyond the courthouse to the county as a whole. His teams deploy agentic AI solutions across county departments, applying the same principles that guided the court work to a broader set of public services. The mandate is the same: use technology to make government more responsive to the people who depend on it.

This book is the account he would have wanted to read before he started. It is written for leaders who need to understand why this technology matters and for practitioners who need to know how to build it right. Both audiences were in the room when he was doing the work. Both deserve an honest account of what he learned.

www.ingramcontent.com/pod-product-compliance
Lightning Source LLC
LaVergne TN
LVHW050937210926
848482LV00013B/647